Department of Political Affairs
Centre for Disarmament Affairs

UNITED NATIONS STANDING ADVISORY COMMITTEE
ON SECURITY QUESTIONS IN CENTRAL AFRICA

United Nations Concern for Peace and Security in Central Africa

Reference Document

United Nations • New York
1997

Note

Financial contributions from Member States, governmental and non-governmental organizations as well as individuals to the Trust Fund set up by the United Nations to support the work of the United Nations Standing Advisory Committee on Security Questions in Central Africa may be forwarded to the Secretary-General of the United Nations. For any other information or enquiries on the Committee and its activities, please contact: Sammy Kum Buo, Secretary, United Nations Standing Advisory Committee on Security Questions in Central Africa, Room 3140E, Department of Political Affairs, United Nations, New York, New York 10017 or through the Internet on: cda@un.org.

UNITED NATIONS PUBLICATION
Sales No. E.98.IX.2
ISBN 92-1-142225-6

TABLE OF CONTENTS

UNITED NATIONS CONCERN FOR PEACE AND SECURITY IN CENTRAL AFRICA

INTRODUCTION

A. Central Africa: hotbed of tension

Central Africa is one of the subregions of the African continent which has been continuously in the headlines for nearly 40 years. Unfortunately, such enduring media attention is more the result of tragedies and recurrent crises than of joyful events. Nearly half of the 11 member countries of the Economic Community of Central African States (ECCAS) have periodically experienced, at various times in the recent past, armed conflicts and the subsequent massive loss of life, considerable displacements of civilian populations, including refugees, and widespread destruction.

It has been estimated that in the first half of the 1990s alone, nearly 5 million people died worldwide as a result of wars and armed conflicts. Africa alone accounted for 3.5 million of those who perished. All evidence points to central Africa as being one of the most affected areas, especially after the large-scale massacres committed between April and July 1994 in Rwanda alone, which reportedly claimed between 500,000 and 1,000,000 lives.

Such tensions and upheavals have consistently hampered economic development and slowed down any momentum towards national and subregional cohesion. Observers unanimously agree that these crises have considerably delayed the emergence of democratic and pluralistic regimes and thus restricted the enjoyment of fundamental human rights and freedoms.

It should be stressed, however, that at the outbreak of every crisis, the countries of the subregion have undertaken political and diplomatic initiatives, sometimes in cooperation with other African states, in an attempt to arrive at a peaceful settlement. In some cases, such initiatives have yielded tangible results. The establishment in May 1997, in the Central African Republic, of the Inter-African Mission to Monitor the Implementation of the Bangui Agreements

(MISAB) and the creation of the International Mediation Committee on the Congo conflict, constitute two recent examples of subregional efforts at crisis management and resolution in central Africa.

The international community, spearheaded by the United Nations, has also been active in support of peace efforts when crises erupt. In central Africa, the United Nations is involved in multifaceted programmes aimed at preventing or curbing conflicts. Whenever open hostilities have broken out, the Security Council and the Organization's specialized agencies and bodies have contributed towards efforts to end the fighting, to reconcile the belligerents, to provide assistance to the affected populations, to restore lasting peace and to contribute to stimulating development and reconstruction upon the restoration of peace.

As part of this active and comprehensive policy of the United Nations in support of central Africa, the Organization put the premises and resources of its Regional Centre for Peace and Disarmament in Africa, located in Lomé, Togo, at the disposal of the central African states for the holding, from 15 to 19 February 1988, of the first conference to examine the interrelated challenges of development, security and confidence-building among the ECCAS States.

That decision, taken at the request of the countries of the subregion, emanated from an initiative by Cameroon which, as the then Chairman of ECCAS, had proposed to the United Nations on 28 November 1986 a programme to identify and implement confidence-building, security and development measures in the central African subregion.

Subsequently, the Secretary-General established, on 28 May 1992, the United Nations Standing Advisory Committee on Security Questions in Central Africa, pursuant to General Assembly resolution 46/37 B of 6 December 1991.

The United Nations Standing Advisory Committee on Security Questions in Central Africa was therefore established as part of the collective efforts of the countries of the subregion, with the United Nations assisting those efforts by providing an appropriate forum and making available to the subregion the long and wide experience of the world body in the field of peace and security.

Since its establishment, the Committee has been involved in developing and promoting measures in the fields of preventive diplomacy, peacemaking and peace-building. The Committee is also involved in the training of peacekeeping personnel of its member states to facilitate more active participation by central African states in peace operations.

One of the most important recent decisions of the Committee was the adoption, in September 1993 in Libreville, of a Non-Aggression Pact. The Pact, which was presented to the Heads of State and Government on 8 July 1996 in Yaoundé for signature, has been signed to date by 9 of the Committee's 11 member countries (Angola and Rwanda have not yet signed the Pact).

B. Historic ties between the United Nations and central Africa

Since its inception, the United Nations has been unwavering in its support of central African countries. Shortly after its creation, at the end of the Second World War, the Organization embarked on the struggle for the decolonization of central African and other African states. It was in that context that the United Nations called for an end to French and United Kingdom trusteeship administration of Cameroon.

When the countries of the subregion (with the exception of Angola) became independent in 1960, they became Members of the United Nations and formed, together with the other newly independent countries of Africa and Asia, the largest group in the General Assembly. As a result of the expansion in the membership of the United Nations, the Organization intensified its actions on behalf of the "third world", focusing increasingly on decolonization and development.

C. Efforts to promote respect for human rights and to eliminate impunity

While the battle for decolonization has, with time, been won, issues relating to human rights and development are still of active current concern. Added to these are other long- or short-term United Nations activities relating to peacekeeping, refugee assistance and support for democratic processes, especially with regard to elections. To this range of missions must be added the adoption of specific measures to eliminate impunity, such as the establishment of the International Criminal Tribunal for the Prosecution of Persons Responsible for Genocide and Other Serious Violations of International Humanitarian Law Committed in the Territory of Rwanda and Rwandan Citizens Responsible for Genocide and Other Such Violations Committed in the Territory of Neighbouring States between 1 January 1994 and 31 December 1994. Created by the Security Council on 8 November 1994, the tribunal, the first such judicial body ever established on the African continent, has been entrusted with the mission of trying those alleged to be responsible for the genocide perpetrated in Rwanda. The Tribunal is based in Arusha, United Republic of Tanzania.

Also within the context of United Nations efforts to eliminate impunity is the commission of investigation established by the Security Council in 1997 to ascertain whether or not civilians had been massacred in the territory of the former Zaire beginning in 1993. It is widely felt that ending impunity is vital not only for assuring the rule of law but also for enhancing prospects for sustainable stability, peace and democracy.

D. Peacekeeping operations in central Africa: 1960-1997

Democratic Republic of the Congo

A few weeks prior to the opening of the fifty-second session of the United Nations General Assembly in September 1997, Mr. Bill Richardson, the United States ambassador to the United Nations, noted that "close to 65 per cent" of the Security Council's work had to do with peace operations in Africa. This remark calls to mind the deplorable recurrence of conflicts on the continent, as well as the search by the United Nations and the international community at large for solutions to these crises.

In the area of peacekeeping, the first United Nations peacekeeping operation in sub-Saharan Africa took place in the Democratic Republic of the Congo, in 1960.

A few days after attaining independence on 30 June 1960, the former Belgian colony was overtaken by a wave of murderous violence. The mineral-rich province of Katanga (now Shaba) in the southern part of the country was threatening to secede. Unable to ensure the security and unity of his country, Congolese Prime Minister Patrice Lumumba turned to the United Nations on 12 July 1960 for military assistance.

On 14 July 1960, the Security Council responded favourably to his request and immediately authorized the formation of the United Nations Operation in the Congo (ONUC). Within two days, United Nations troops, contributed by many countries (mostly in Africa and Asia), began arriving in the Congo.

Between July 1960 and June 1964, nearly 20,000 troops and civilians were mobilized for ONUC under the flag of the Organization. The operation cost the United Nations more than $400 million at the time, and was also marked by the deaths of 245 "Blue Helmets" and 5 international civilian experts. These losses are enormous when compared to the total of 1,194 staff members killed in all United Nations peacekeeping operations throughout the world between 1948 and 1994.

A particularly tragic loss during the ONUC operation was the death of Dag Hammarskjöld in a "mysterious plane accident" on 18 September 1961 on the border between the Congo and Northern Rhodesia (now Zambia). The death of the Organization's second Secretary-General in dramatic circumstances was met with great emotion in Central Africa and throughout the world. For many, he had embodied more than anyone the United Nations' ceaseless quest for peace.

The Democratic Republic of the Congo was once again a theatre of large-scale armed conflict between October 1996 and May 1997. The United Nations, in close cooperation with the OAU, again undertook significant mediation activities in an attempt to restore peace. Within the framework of this initiative, the Secretaries-General of the United Nations and of the OAU appointed Mr. Mohamed Sahnoun as joint Special Representative for the Great Lakes region.

Republic of the Congo

In June 1997, following the outbreak of a new political and military conflict in Brazzaville in the Republic of the Congo, the joint United Nations/OAU Special Representative for the Great Lakes region was asked to assist President Omar Bongo of Gabon in his leadership of an international committee to mediate the conflict.

The Security Council also received a request from President Omar Bongo of Gabon in his capacity as Chairman of the international mediation committee calling for a United Nations peacekeeping force to be sent to the Republic of the Congo, and the Secretary-General responded by sending a team to Brazzaville and to neighbouring countries to study the feasibility of such an operation. No final decision regarding the force had been taken by the Security Council at the time this report was prepared. As with all armed conflicts, no peace arrangement imposed from outside can succeed without the agreement of the parties to the conflict to pursue a peaceful negotiated solution. In October 1997, the Congolese armed conflict reached a decisive stage with the return to power of former President Denis Sassou Nguessou.

Angola

In the area of United Nations peacekeeping operations in central Africa, Angola has received continuous assistance from the United Nations since 1989. Three United Nations Angola Verification Missions (UNAVEM I, UNAVEM II, and UNAVEM III) were established there between January 1989 and June 1997.

The civil conflict in Angola broke out with the attainment of independence by this former Portuguese colony on 11 November 1975. The conflict would pit two former liberation movements, MPLA, the party in power, and UNITA, against each other. The two movements waged a fratricidal war with the support of outside Powers. This occurred at the height of the cold war, at a time when international relations were often determined on the basis of East/West rivalry.

In December 1988, the first glimmers of hope for peace in Angola emerged with the adoption of a tripartite agreement between Angola, Cuba and South Africa, embodying their mutual commitment to a withdrawal of foreign military forces from Angolan territory. This decisive step forward was achieved as a result of diplomatic efforts of the United States and the United Nations. On 31 May 1991, a new stage was reached in the quest for peace with the signing of the peace accords between the Government of Angola and UNITA at Bicesse in Portugal. Immediately thereafter, the Government of Angola requested the United Nations to undertake to verify the implementation of the accords. In 1992, the Security Council expanded the United Nations role in Angola to include monitoring the elections envisaged by the peace process.

In September 1992, the first round of legislative and presidential elections was held. The results of the voting were published on 17 October by the National Electoral Commission. These results, which were broadly favourable to MPLA, were rejected by UNITA. In spite of the Security Council's urgent appeals to both sides in Angola to accept the outcome of the voting, hostilities resumed on 30 October 1992.

Full-scale peace negotiations between the Government of Angola and UNITA under United Nations auspices would not resume until 15 November 1993. One year later, on 20 November 1994, the final peace agreements between the Angolan parties were signed in

Lusaka, Zambia, once again under the auspices of the United Nations.

More than 9,000 United Nations "Blue Helmets", police personnel and civilian experts were deployed in Angola between 1989 and 1997. The financial cost to the United Nations of this long-term operation has already passed the $1 billion mark.

In June 1997, the United Nations Observer Mission in Angola (MONUA) took over from the preceding verification missions. The structure of this Mission includes military, police and civilian personnel. The tasks entrusted to MONUA by the Security Council comprise assistance in the final implementation of the provisions of the Lusaka Agreements, electoral assistance, humanitarian assistance and help in rebuilding the country.

Rwanda

The conflict in Rwanda, which culminated in 1994 in the large-scale massacres that have since been termed genocide, forms part of a crisis that goes back to 1990. During that year, sporadic fighting occurred regularly between government forces and the forces of the Rwandese Patriotic Front (RPF) operating out of the northern part of the country. Since independence, the country's Hutu and Tutsi communities have regularly clashed in confrontations of this kind, against a backdrop of political and ethnic animosities.

On 22 June 1993, following an upsurge in tension, the Security Council established the United Nations Observer Mission Uganda-Rwanda (UNOMUR). Subsequently, with the support of the United Nations and countries of the subregion and East Africa, inter-Rwandese peace talks produced the peace agreements that were signed at Arusha in the United Republic of Tanzania. The Office of the United Nations High Commissioner for Refugees took advantage of this lull in the conflict to assist some 600,000 Rwandese refugees in neighbouring countries to return to their own country.

At the request of the Government of Rwanda and the Rwandese Patriotic Front, the Security Council established the United Nations Assistance Mission for Rwanda (UNAMIR) on 5 October 1993.

UNAMIR, whose personnel numbered as many as 5,500, mostly military personnel, entailed expenditure by the United Nations of more than $437 million between October 1993 and March 1996.

The efforts of the United Nations, of the international community at large and of the States of the subregion to prevent the situation in Rwanda from escalating after the Arusha agreement would prove to be unavailing. Between April and July 1994, clashes once again broke out following the death of the Head of State of Rwanda, Juvénal Habiyarimana, in a plane crash over Kigali airport, which occurred in conditions that are still shrouded in mystery. Parallel to the fighting between government and RPF forces, targeted massacres were perpetrated throughout the country by government forces and by their militia and civilian allies, often armed with machetes.

In the aftermath of this painful tragedy, the United Nations made two fund-raising appeals for humanitarian assistance to and the reconstruction of Rwanda. In addition, the decision to establish the International Criminal Tribunal to try persons suspected of being responsible for war crimes was taken by the Security Council.

After the final withdrawal of UNAMIR in March 1996, several hundred thousand Rwandese who had fled to the eastern part of the former Zaire began returning to their country in October 1996, following the launching of a counter-offensive against the regime of ex-President Mobutu by the forces of the Democratic Alliance. Following the large-scale return of refugees, the humanitarian and human rights situation in Rwanda has increasingly attracted international attention.

Burundi

Burundi too has been the theatre of violent political and ethnic conflicts which also pit Hutu against Tutsi and also date back to the independence of this former Belgian colony.

The most recent major armed upheaval occurred in 1993 following the assassination of the first democratically elected Hutu Head of State in the history of Burundi, Melchior Ndadaye. Since that time, it is estimated that over 150,000 Burundians have been killed in sporadic outbursts of violence and armed confrontations punctuated by various atrocities, by the mass flight of citizens to other countries, the forced internal displacement of inhabitants and numerous human rights violations.

The Office of the United Nations High Commissioner for Human Rights has an observer mission in Burundi. Humanitarian agencies such as the Office of the United Nations High Commissioner for Refugees and the World Food Programme are working tirelessly to carry out humanitarian programmes benefiting several million civilians.

With regard to peace efforts, a Special Representative of the United Nations Secretary-General was first posted to Bujumbura in 1993 and the office has continued to operate there. The United Nations, and in particular the Security Council, continue to follow closely developments in Burundi. The United Nations is also closely associated with the efforts of the countries of the subregion and countries of East Africa to bring about lasting peace in Burundi.

Chad

The involvement of the United Nations in Chad in the context of a peacekeeping operation was brief but completely successful. The United Nations Aouzou Strip Observer Group (UNASOG) operated between May and June 1994. Comprising nine military officers, the Group's role was to verify the withdrawal of the Libyan administration from the Aouzou Strip, which had been recognized as being an integral part of Chad's national territory.

Before the dispute was settled peacefully by the International Court of Justice in The Hague, Chad and the Libyan Arab Jamahiriya quarrelled over this region for several years, often resorting to force in an attempt to settle the dispute.

UNASOG, which lasted one month, cost the United Nations approximately $67,000.

CONCLUSION

The above introductory presentation and the reference document as a whole demonstrate the interest which the United Nations has consistently shown in promoting lasting solutions to the various crises in central Africa. In its work in the area, the United Nations maintains close cooperation with the member states of the Economic Community of Central African States (ECCAS). This arrangement has allowed the subregional community to turn to the United Nations for support and assistance in the development of relations based on mutual trust and peaceful cooperation.

This synergy for peace and security between the countries of central Africa and the United Nations, increasingly channelled, since 1992, within the framework of the activities of the United Nations Standing Advisory Committee on Security Questions in Central Africa, is undoubtedly destined to develop further and to grow stronger in the future as central African states strive to move away from conflict towards sustainable peace and development.

New York, December 1997

Basic Facts on the
United Nations Standing Advisory Committee
on Security Questions in Central Africa

> "...peace and security, in central Africa or anywhere cannot be imposed from outside. The primary responsibility rests with the leaders of the countries concerned.
>
> The United Nations General Assembly was not mistaken in seeing your Committee as an essential instrument for the building of peace and trust among your States.
>
> On behalf of the United Nations, let me assure you sincerely once again of our full support and cooperation."
>
> **Kofi A. Annan**
> **Secretary-General of the United Nations**
> **7 July 1997**

What is the Standing Advisory Committee?

The Standing Advisory Committee is a subregional grouping of eleven United Nations Member States that are also members of the Economic Community of Central African States (ECCAS). It was created to develop confidence-building measures and to encourage arms limitation and development in the Central African subregion. It was conceived as an instrument of preventive diplomacy aimed at avoiding conflicts within and between its member States.

The Committee was established by the United Nations Secretary-General on 28 May 1992 in response to General Assembly resolution 46/37 B. By the resolution, the Assembly supported and encouraged efforts to further disarmament and non-proliferation measures at regional and subregional levels and welcomed the initiative taken by the States of the Central African subregion in recommending the creation of such a Committee.

How is the Committee organized?

The Committee meets twice a year: on each occasion, it meets first at the expert level, with senior military and civilian officials, and then at the ministerial level, with ministers of defence and of foreign affairs participating. It also meets at the level of Heads of State and Government.

The leadership of the Committee is exercised through an elected Bureau composed of a President, two Vice-Presidents and a Rapporteur. The current members of the Bureau, elected at the Ninth Ministerial meeting in July 1997 in Libreville, as follows: President: Gabon; First Vice-President: Angola; Second Vice-President: Chad; Rapporteur: Burundi. Sammy Kum Buo, Senior Political Affairs Officer in the Centre for Disarmament Affairs of the Department of Political Affairs in the United Nations Secretariat is the Secretary of the Committee.

Who else participates in the Committee's work?

The Committee has adopted the following principles concerning observers at its meetings:

1. With respect to subregional organizations for economic development and the Organization of African Unity (OAU). The Committee grants these bodies the status of permanent observer.

2. Other States Members of the United Nations, international organizations and non-governmental organizations, research institutes and any individual concerned with promoting international peace and security may participate in meetings upon request and with the agreement of the Bureau of the Committee.

3. Furthermore, as appropriate, the Committee may invite any individual, in his or her capacity as expert or consultant, to participate in its meetings.

What does the Committee do?

Programme of work

The overall aim of the Committee is to elaborate, adopt and implement specific confidence-building measures for the subregion. At its first session, held at Yaoundé in July 1992, it decided to focus on such measures as the following:

Immediate measures:
Preventive diplomacy
- Adherence by all States of the subregion to international legal instruments on arms limitation and disarmament.

- Encouragement and promotion of the policy of voluntary repatriation of refugees and application of practical measures to enable them to reintegrate into society, as a humanitarian element of confidence-building.

- Conclusion of a subregional non-aggression pact. Work on this measure was completed when the text of the pact was unanimously adopted at the ministerial meeting of the Committee held in Libreville in September 1993. The formal signature of the Pact by the Heads of State and Government took place on 8 July 1996 in Yaounde, Cameroon.

- Organization of regular joint meetings of ministers of defence, of the interior and for foreign affairs, as well as of chiefs of staff of the armed forces and police forces of the subregion.

- Establishment and improvement of transparency in military activities, including prior notification to other States of the subregion of each State's military exercises, and invitation to other States of the subregion to observe such exercises.

- Agreement on the part of all States in the subregion not to produce, acquire or transfer weapons of mass destruction, such as nuclear, chemical and biological weapons.

Peace-building
- Strengthening and consolidation of the democratization process and promotion of respect for human rights and the rule of law in each State in the subregion.

- Establishment of a crisis-management body in each member State.

- Increased involvement of the civil society and the population as a whole in the pursuit of the ideals of peace, security and development in the subregion.

- Adoption of measures to promote awareness among potential emigrants or immigrants of the laws and the culture of receiving countries, and increased cooperation in the area of emigration and immigration through the drafting or implementation of subregional legislation on the movement of persons.

- Expansion of cooperation and exchange programmes in the fields of information, culture and education.

- Exchange of military delegations.

- Elaboration of specific measures for promoting agreement on a balanced and gradual reduction of the military forces, equipment and budgets of the States of the subregion.

- Assistance in connection with the restructuring of armies and redeployment of military resources.

Peacemaking and peace-keeping
- Establishment of a standing inter-State mechanism for crisis management and preventive early warning.

- Development of cooperation to enhance training of military and civilian personnel for peacekeeping and other peace operations.

Compliance and verification
- Establishment of appropriate verification measures in conjunction with the confidence-building and security measures mentioned above.

Long-term measures:
Preventive diplomacy
- Expansion of each State's diplomatic presence in the other countries of the subregion.

- Strengthening of subregional cooperation in the field of military training.

- Organization of joint military exercises and joint military patrols.

- Training, at the subregional level, in the management of emergency humanitarian assistance operations.

- Establishment of units for peace operations within the armed forces of each member state.

Peace-building
- The strengthening of cooperation between neighbouring countries through the creation of markets and other joint economic development projects in border zones and expansion of contacts between border authorities.

- Development of means of transport and communication between States of the subregion.

- Creation of demilitarized zones and zones of peace.

Some recent decisions of the Committee

1. To promote agreement on a balanced and gradual reduction of the military forces. equipment and budgets of member States.

2. To promote the establishment of a standing inter-State mechanism for crisis management.

3. To create specialized units for peace-keeping operations within their respective armed forces.

4. To participate more actively in peace-keeping, humanitarian and other peace operations organized under the auspices of the United Nations and/or the OAU.

5. To enhance subregional efforts to combat the illicit transfer and acquisition of arms and drugs.

6. To promote programmes for the retraining and reintegration into civilian life of demobilized soldiers and militias in the countries of the subregion.

What has the Committee achieved?

1.   Since its establishment in 1992, the Committee has successfully negotiated and concluded a Non-Aggression Pact among its member States. The Pact has formally been signed so far by nine of the eleven member states. The Pact aims to prevent future inter-state conflicts and to strengthen confidence and cooperation among member states.

2.   The Committee has adopted a typology of sources of internal and inter-state conflict in the subregion. The document lists potential areas of crises, thus making it easier to focus on preventive efforts.

3.   On 8 July 1996, in Yaounde, member states held their first ever summit conference to consider the security situation in central Africa and to sign the Non-Aggression Pact. They also adopted a Final Declaration in which they undertook to implement specific measures at the internal and inter-state levels to promote prospects for confidence-building and sustainable peace and progress. The Heads of State and Government also agreed to meet periodically to examine issues of peace and security in their subregion and, in this connection held an extraordinary summit in Brazzaville on 2 and 3 December 1996 to discuss the various crises in the Great Lakes, especially the situation at the time in the former Zaire. The idea of regular summit gatherings has been welcomed as a constructive confidence-building measure as such meetings provide valuable opportunities for leaders, even those whose countries may be in conflict, to initiate or strengthen dialogue with a view to solving their disputes through peaceful means.

4.   In September 1996, with a grant from the Government of Japan, the Committee organized at Yaounde the first training seminar on peace operations for senior military and civilian officials of the eleven member states of the Committee. The objective was to launch a programme to enhance the capacity of central African countries to participate more actively in future United Nations and/or OAU peace operations, especially in the subregion.

5.   The Committee has launched a fundraising appeal to generate the necessary resources for the effective establishment and functioning of its Early Warning Mechanism for Central Africa. The Mechanism, which central African leaders decided should be set up in Libreville, will be financed from voluntary contributions.

"The United Nations has had much to say about conventional arms. But has the time not arrived for some practical and verifiable measures in this field? More confidence-building measures, particularly at the regional level, are needed.

I am in full support, for example, of the work of the Standing Advisory Committee on Security Questions in Central Africa -- grouping of 11 States. Their non-aggression treaty should provide a model of a regional confidence-building measure."

Boutros Boutros-Ghali
Secretary-General of the United Nations
Geneva, 12 January 1994

Country Profiles of Central African States*

Angola

General Information
UN membership date:	1 December 1976
Population:	11,072,000 (1995 est..)
Surface area:	1,246,700 sq km
Border countries:	Congo, Namibia, Zaire, Zambia
Official language(s):	Portuguese
Currency:	new kwanza (NKz)

Economic Indicators
GDP (million US$):	5,954	(1991)
GDP (per capita US$):	625	(1991)

Social Indicators
Growth rate of population (% per annum):	3.7	(1990/95)
Age group 0-14 years (%):	47.1	(1990/95)
Age group 60+ years (women/men,%):	2.5/2.1	(1990/95)
Life expectancy at birth (women/men, years):	48/45	(1990/95)
Infant mortality rate (per 1,000 births):	124	(1990/95)
Refugees:	11,000	(1990/95)

Major Resources
Petroleum, diamonds, iron ore, phosphates, copper, feldspar, gold, bauxite, uranium.

Burundi

General Information
UN membership date:	18 September 1962
Population:	6,343,000 (1995 est.)
Surface area:	27,834 sq km
Border countries:	Democratic Republic of the Congo, Rwanda, Tanzania
Official language(s):	Kirundi, French
Currency:	Burundi franc

Economic Indicators
GDP (million US$):	1,170	(1991)
GDP (per capita US$):	207	(1991)

Social Indicators
Growth rate of population (% per annum):	2.9	(1990/95)
Age group 0-14 years (%):	46.3	(1990/95)
Age group 60+ years (women/men,%):	2.6/1.8	(1990/95)
Life expectancy at birth (women/men, years):	50/46	(1990/95)
Infant mortality rate (per 1,000 births):	106	(1990/95)
Refugees:	271,700	(1990/95)

Major Resources
Nickel, uranium, rare earth oxides, peat, cobalt, copper, platinum (not yet exploited), vanadium.

Cameroon

General Information
UN membership date:	20 September 1960
Population:	13,275,000
Surface area:	475,442 sq km
Border countries:	Central African Republic, Chad, Congo, Equatorial Guinea, Gabon, Nigeria,
Official language(s):	English, French
Currency:	CFA franc

Economic Indicators
GDP (million US$):	12,788	(1991)
GDP (per capita US$):	1,079	(1991)

Social Indicators
Growth rate of population (% per annum):	2.8	(1990/95)
Age group 0-14 years (%):	44.0	(1990/95)
Age group 60+ years (women/men, %):	3.0/2.5	(1990/95)
Life expectancy at birth (women/men, years):	58/55	(1990/95)
Infant mortality rate (per 1,000 births):	63	(1990/95)
Refugees:	42,200	(1990/95)

Major Resources
Petroleum, bauxite, iron ore, timber, hydropower potential.

Central African Republic

General Information
UN membership date:	20 September 1960
Population:	3,429,000
Surface area:	622,984 sp km
Border countries:	Cameroon, Chad, Congo, Democratic Republic of the Congo, Sudan
Official language(s):	French
Currency:	CFA franc

Economic Indicators
GDP (million US$):	1,443	(1991)
GDP (per capita US$):	467	(1991)

Social Indicators
Growth rate of population (% per annum):	2.6	(1990/95)
Age group 0-14 years (%):	45.2	(1990/95)
Age group 60+ years (women/men, %):	3.3/2.5	(1990/95)
Life expectancy at birth (women/men, years):	49/45	(1990/95)
Infant mortality rate (per 1,000 births):	105	(1990/95)
Refugees:	19,000	(1990/95)

Major Resources
Diamonds, uranium, timber, gold, oil.

---

* Information drawn from <u>World Statistics Pocketbook 1995</u>, United Nations publication, (Sales No. E.95.XVII.7) and other public documents.

Chad

General Information
UN membership date:	20 September 1960
Population:	6,361,000
Surface area:	1,284,000 sq km
Border countries:	Cameroon, Central African Republic, Libya, Niger, Nigeria, Sudan
Official language(s):	French, Arabic
Currency:	CFA franc

Economic Indicators
GDP (million US$):	1,290	(1991)
GDP (per capita US$):	227	(1991)

Social Indicators
Growth rate of population (% per annum):	2.7	(1990/95)
Age group 0-14 years (%):	43.4	(1990/95)
Age group 60+ years (women/men, %):	3.1/2.5	(1990/95)
Life expectancy at birth (women/men, years):	49/46	(1990/95)
Infant mortality rate (per 1,000 births):	122	(1990/95)
Refugees:	--	

Major Resources
Petroleum (unexploited but exploration under way), uranium, natron, kaolin, fish (Lake Chad).

-- data not available or not applicable

Democratic Republic of the Congo

General Information
UN membership date:	20 September 1960
Population:	43,814,000 (1995)
Surface area:	2,344,858 sq km
Border countries:	Angola, Burundi, Central African Republic, Congo, Rwanda, Sudan, Uganda, Zambia
Official language(s):	French
Currency:	zaire

Economic Indicators
GDP (million US$):	3,594	(1991)
GDP (per capita US$):	93	(1991)

Social Indicators
Growth rate of population (% per annum):	3.2	(1990/95)
Age group 0-14 years (%):	48.1	(1990/95)
Age group 60+ years (women/men, %):	2.6/2.0	(1990/95)
Life expectancy at birth (women/men, years):	53/50	(1990/95)
Infant mortality rate (per 1,000 births):	93	(1990/95)
Refugees:	391,100	(1990/95)

Major Resources
Cobalt, copper, cadmium, petroleum, industrial and gem diamonds, gold, silver, zinc, manganese, tin, germanium, uranium, radium, bauxite, iron ore, coal, hydropower potential.

Congo

General Information
UN membership date:	20 September 1960
Population:	2,590,000
Surface area:	342,000 sq km
Border countries:	Angola, Cameroon, Central African Republic, Democratic Republic of the Congo, Gabon
Official language(s):	French
Currency:	CFA franc

Economic Indicators
GDP (million US$):	2,909 (1991)
GDP (per capita US$):	1,266 (1991)

Social Indicators
Growth rate of population (% per annum):	3.0	(1990/95)
Age group 0-14 years (%):	45.7	(1990/95)
Age group 60+ years (women/men, %):	2.8/2.3	(1990/95)
Life expectancy at birth (women/men, years):	54/49	(1990/95)
Infant mortality rate (per 1,000 births):	82	(1990/95)
Refugees:	9,500	(1990/95)

Major Resources
Petroleum, timber, potash, lead, zinc, uranium, copper, phosphates, natural gas.

Equatorial Guinea

General Information
UN membership date:	12 November 1968
Population:	400,000 (1995)
Surface area:	28,051 sq km
Border countries:	Cameroon, Gabon
Official language(s):	Spanish
Currency:	CFA franc

Economic Indicators
GDP (million US$):	165 (1991)
GDP (per capita US$):	457 (1991)

Social Indicators
Growth rate of population (% per annum):	2.6	1990/95
Age group 0-14 years (%):	43.3	(1990/95)
Age group 60+ years (women/men, %):	3.8/2.8	(1990/95)
Life expectancy at birth (women/men, years):	50/46	(1990/95)
Infant mortality rate (per 1,000 births):	117	(1990/95)
Refugees:	--	

Major Resources
Timber, petroleum, small unexploited deposits of gold, manganese, uranium.

-- data not available or not applicable

Gabon

General Information
UN membership date:	20 September 1960
Population:	1,367,000 (1995 est.)
Surface area:	267,667 sq km
Border countries:	Cameroon, Congo, Equatorial Guinea
Official language(s):	French
Currency:	CFA franc

Economic Indicators
GDP (million US$):	4,438 (1991)
GDP (per capita US$):	3,708 (1991)

Social Indicators
Growth rate of population (% per annum):	3.3	(1990/95)
Age group 0-14 years (%):	35.9	(1990/95)
Age group 60+ years (women/men, %):	5.0/4.0	(1990/95)
Life expectancy at birth (women/men, years):	55/52	(1990/95)
Infant mortality rate (per 1,000 births):	94	(1990/95)
Refugees:	300	(1990/95)

Major Resources
Petroleum, manganese, uranium, gold, timber, iron ore.

Rwanda

General Information
UN membership date:	18 September 1962
Population:	8,330,000 (1995 est.)
Surface area:	26,338 sq km
Border countries:	Burundi, Democratic Republic of the Congo, Tanzania, Uganda
Official language(s):	Kinyarwanda, French, English
Currency:	Rwanda franc

Economic Indicators
GDP (million US$):	1,701 (1991)
GDP (per capita US$):	234 (1991)

Social Indicators
Growth rate of population (% per annum):	3.4	(1990/95)
Age group 0-14 years (%):	49.8	(1990/95)
Age group 60+ years (women/men, %):	2.0/1.7	(1990/95)
Life expectancy at birth (women/men, years):	48/45	(1990/95)
Infant mortality rate (per 1,000 births):	110	(1990/95)
Refugees:	25,200	(1990/95)

Major Resources
Gold, cassiterite (tin ore), wolframite (tungsten ore), natural gas, hydropower.

Sao Tome and Principe

General Information
UN membership date:	16 September 1975
Population:	97,000 (1995 est.)
Surface area:	964 sq km
Border countries:	
Official language(s):	Portuguese
Currency:	dobra

Economic Indicators
GDP (million US$):	45 (1991)
GDP (per capita US$):	373 (1991)

Social Indicators
Growth rate of population (% per annum):	--	
Age group 0-14 years (%):	46.3	(1980)
Age group 60+ years (women/men, %):	3.9/3.2	(1981)
Life expectancy at birth (women/men, years):	--	
Infant mortality rate (per 1,000 births):	72	(1990/95)
Refugees:	--	

Major Resources
Fish.

-- data not available or not applicable

United Nations Peacekeeping and Other United Nations Peace Missions in Central Africa*

ANGOLA

■ UNAVEM I
United Nations Angola Verification Mission I

Duration: January 1989 - 25 May 1991
Location: Angola
Headquarters: Luanda
Strength: 70 military observers, supported by international and locally recruited civilian staff
Fatalities: None
Expenditures: $16,404,200
Authorization: S/RES/626 on 20 December 1988
Function: Established to verify the redeployment of Cuban troops northward and their phased and total withdrawal from the territory of Angola in accordance with the timetable agreed between Angola and Cuba.

■ UNAVEM II
United Nations Angola Verification Mission II

Duration: 30 May 1991 - February 1995
Location: Angola
Headquarters: Luanda
Strength: 350 military observers, 126 police monitors, some 80 international civilian staff and 155 local staff, and up to 400 electoral observers
Fatalities: 5 (2 military observers, 1 other military personnel, 1 police observer and 1 international civilian staff)
Expenditures: $175,802,600
Special Representative of the Secretary-General and Chief of Mission: Mr. Alioune Blondin Beye (Mali)
Chief Military Observer: Major-General Chris Abutu Garuba (Nigeria)
Authorization: S/RES/696 on 30 May 1991
Function: Established to verify the arrangements agreed by the Angolan parties for the monitoring of the cease-fire and for the monitoring of the Angolan police during the cease-fire period and to observer and verify the elections in that country, in accordance with the Peace Accords for Angola, signed by the Angolan government and the União Nacional para a Independência Total de Angola (UNITA). Despite the United Nations verification that the elections -- held in September 1992 -- had been generally free and fair, their results were contested by UNITA. After renewed fighting in October 1992 between the government and UNITA forces, UNAVEM II's mandate was adjusted in order to help the two sides reach agreement on modalities for completing the peace process and, at the same time, to broker and help implement cease-fires at the national or local level. Following the signing on 20 November 1994 by the Government of Angola and UNITA of the Lusaka Protocol, UNAVEM II verified the initial stages of the peace agreement.

■ UNAVEM III
United Nations Angola Verification Mission III

Duration: February 1995 to 30 June 1997
Location: Angola
Headquarters: Luanda
Authorized Strength: 350 military observers, 7,000 other military personnel, 260 police observers, 336 international civilian staff, 343 locally recruited staff and 68 United Nations volunteers
Strength (as of 30 June 1997): 283 military observers, 3,649 troops and 288 civilian police

---

* Information drawn from United Nations Department of Public Information publications.

Fatalities: 32
Expenditures: $887,196,700
Special Representative of the Secretary-General and Chief of Mission:
Mr. Alioune Blondin Beye (Mali)
Force Commander: Major-General Phillip Valerio Sibanda (Zimbabwe)
Authorization: S/RES/976 on
8 February 1995
Function: Established to assist the government of Angola and the UNITA in restoring peace and achieving national reconciliation on the basis of the "Accordos de Paz" signed 31 May 1991, the Lusaka Protocol signed on 20 November 1994, and relevant Security Council resolutions. Among the main features of UNAVEM III's mandate are the following: to provide good offices and meditation to the Angolan parties; to monitor and verify the extension of State administration throughout the country and the process of national reconciliation; to supervise, control and verify the disengagement of forces and to monitor the cease-fire; to verify information receive from the government and UNITA regarding their forces, as well as all troop movements; to assist in the establishment of quartering areas; to verify the withdrawal, quartering and demobilization of UNITA forces; to supervise the collection and storage of UNITA armaments; to verify the movement of government forces (FAA) to barracks and the completion of the formation of FAA; to verify the free circulation of persons and goods; to verify and monitor the neutrality of the Angolan National Police, the disarming of civilians, the quartering of the rapid reaction police, and security arrangements for UNITA leaders; to coordinate, facilitate and support humanitarian activities directly linked to the peace process, as well as participating in mine-clearance activities; to declare formally that all essential requirements for the holding of the second round of presidential elections have been fulfilled, and to support, verify and monitor the electoral process.

■ MONUA
United Nations Observer Mission in Angola

Duration: July 1997 to present
Location: Angola
Headquarters: Luanda
Authorized Strength: 193 military contingent personnel, 86 military observers and 345 civilian police monitors, supported by some 310 international civilian staff
Current Strength: 3,568 (as UNAVEM III draws down)
Special Representative of the Secretary-General and Chief of Mission:
Mr. Alioune Blondin Beye (Mali)
Force Commander: Major-General Phillip Valerio Sibanda (Zimbabwe)
Authorization: S/RES/1118 on
30 June 1997
Function: Established as a follow on mission to succeed UNAVEM III, MONUA is to assist the Angolan parties in consolidating peace and national reconciliation, enhancing confidence-building and creating an environment conducive to long-term stability, democratic development and rehabilitation of the country. The initial mandate of MONUA extended to 31 October 1997, and it was subsequently renewed until 31 January 1998. MONUA is mandated to work towards completion of the demobilization process, incorporation of ex-combatants of UNITA into the Angolan Armed Forces (FAA) and the Angolan National Police, integration of UNITA personnel in all levels of State administration, elimination of all the impediments to free circulation of people and goods, as well as the disarmament of the civilian population.

BURUNDI

■ Special Representative for Burundi

On 17 November 1993, Secretary-General Boutros Boutros-Ghali designated Mr. Ahmedou Ould Abdallah, a national of Mauritania, as Special Representative for Burundi. Mr. Abdallah served in that capacity until October 1995. He was succeeded by Mr. Marc Faguy, a national of Canada, who served from January 1996 to February 1997. Mr. Cheikh Tidiane Sy, a national of Senegal, is the current Officer-in-Charge.

CENTRAL AFRICAN REPUBLIC

■ MISAB **
Inter-African Mission to Monitor the Implementation of the Bangui Agreements

Following mediation efforts by a number of African countries led by Burkina Faso, Chad, Gabon and Mali to put an end to the military mutinies that had produced much destruction and violence in the Central Africa Republic in 1996, a peace agreement was reached on 25 January 1997. That agreement included a provision for the deployment of an inter-african peace force called MISAB (Inter-African Mission to Monitor the Implementation of the Bangui Agreements) made up of about 800 troops from Burkina Faso, Chad, Gabon, Mali, Senegal and Togo. Although MISAB was not a United Nations operation, the Security Council in 1997 adopted resolutions S/Res/1125 of 6 August 1997 and S/Res/1136 of 6 November 1997 supporting the mission. On 4 December 1997, a multi-sectoral United Nations team composed of representatives of the Departments of Political Affairs and Peace-keeping Operations as well as of UNDP and UNHCR

** Although MISAB was not a United Nations operation, the Security Council in 1997 adopted resolutions S/Res/1125 and S/Res/1136 supporting the mission.

visited the Central African Republic to assess progress in the implementation of the Bangui Agreements as well as further requirements for the consolidation of peace and security.

CHAD

■ UNASOG
United Nations Aouzou Strip Observer Group

Duration: May 1994 - June 1994
Location: Aouzou Strip, Republic of Chad
Strength: 9 military observers and 6 international civilian staff
Fatalities: None
Expenditures: $67,471
Authorization: S/RES/915 on 5 May 1994
Function: Established to verify the withdrawal of the Libyan administration and forces from the Aouzou Strip in accordance with the decision of the International Court of Justice. UNASOG accomplished its mandate after both sides -- the Republic of Chad and the Libyan Arab Jamahiriya -- declared withdrawal to be complete.

DEMOCRATIC REPUBLIC OF THE CONGO

■ ONUC
United Nations Operation in the Congo

Duration: July 1960 - June 1964
Location: Democratic Republic of the Congo
Headquarters: Léopoldville (now Kinshasa)
Strength: 19,828 military personnel, supported by international and locally recruited civilian staff
Fatalities: 250 (245 military personnel and 5 international civilian staff)
Expenditures: $400,130,793
Authorization: S/RES/143 on 14 July 1960
Function: Initially established to ensure the withdrawal of Belgian forces, to assist the government in maintaining law and order and to provide technical assistance. The function of ONUC was subsequently

modified to include maintaining the territorial integrity and political independence of the Democratic Republic of the Congo, preventing the occurrence of civil war and securing the removal from the Congo of all foreign military, paramilitary and advisory personnel not under the United Nations Command, and all mercenaries.

■ Special Representative for the Great Lakes region

In January 1997, Secretary-General Kofi Annan nominated Mr. Mohamed Sahnoun, a national of Algeria, as United Nations/ Organization of African Unity (OAU) Special Representative for the Great Lakes region. In this capacity, Mr. Sahnoun, among other things, represented the UN and OAU Secretaries-General in the peace efforts related to the 1996/1997 crises in former Zaire, now the Democratic Republic of the Congo.

RWANDA

■ UNOMUR
United Nations Observer Mission Uganda-Rwanda

Duration: June 1993 - October 1993 (officially closed 21 September 1994)
Location: Ugandan side of the Uganda-Rwanda border
Headquarters: Kabale, Uganda
Strength: 81 military observers, supported by international and locally recruited civilian staff
Fatalities: None
Estimated expenditures (from inception to 21 December 1993): $2,298,500 *(after that date, the costs related to UNOMUR were reflected in the costs of UNAMIR)*
Authorization: S/RES/846 on 22 June 1993
Function: Established to monitor the border between Uganda and Rwanda and verify that no military assistance -- lethal weapons, ammunition and other material of possible military use -- was being provided across it.

■ UNAMIR
United Nations Assistance Mission for Rwanda

Duration: October 1993 - March 1996
Location: Rwanda
Headquarters: Kigali
Maximum Authorized Strength: Some 5,500 military personnel, including approx. 5,200 troops and military support personnel and 320 military observers, and 120 civilian police personnel; there is also a provision for international and locally recruited civilian staff
Fatalities: 26 (3 military observers, 22 other military personnel and 1 civilian police)
Expenditures (from inception to 19 April 1996): $437,430,100
Special Representative of the Secretary-General and Head of Mission: Mr. Shaharyar M. Khan (Pakistan) succeeded Mr. Jacques-Roger Booh-Booh (Cameroon) who served from October 1993 to June 1994
Force Commander: Major-General Guy Tousignant (Canada) succeeded Major-General Romeo A. Dallaire (Canada) who served from October 1993 to August 1994
Authorization: S/RES/872 on 5 October 1993
Function: Originally established to help implement the Arusha Peace Agreement signed by the Rwandese parties on 4 August 1993. UNAMIR's mandate was: to assist in ensuring the security of the capital city of Kigali; monitor the cease-fire agreement, including establishment of an expanded demilitarized zone and demobilization procedures; monitor the security situation during the final period of the transitional government's mandate leading up to elections; assist with mine-clearance; and assist in the coordination of humanitarian assistance activities in conjunction with relief operations. After renewed fighting in April 1994, the mandate of UNAMIR was adjusted and expanded by Security Council resolution 918 of 17 May 1994 so that it could act as an intermediary between the warring Rwandese parties in

an attempt to secure their agreement to a cease-fire; assist in the resumption of humanitarian relief operations to the extent feasible; and monitor developments in Rwanda, including the safety and security of civilians who sought refuge with UNAMIR. After the situation in Rwanda deteriorated further, UNAMIR's mandate was expanded to enable it to contribute to the security and protection of refugees and civilians at risk, through means including the establishment and maintenance of security humanitarian areas, and the provision of security for relief operations to the degree possible.

Following the cease-fire and the installation of the new government, the tasks of UNAMIR were further adjusted: to ensure stability and security in the north-western and south-western regions of Rwanda; to stabilize and monitor the situation in all regions of Rwanda to encourage the return of the displaced population; to provide security and support for humanitarian assistance operations inside Rwanda; and to promote, through mediation and good offices, national reconciliation in Rwanda. UNAMIR also contributed to the security in Rwanda of personnel of the International Tribunal for Rwanda and of human rights officers, and assisted in the establishment and training of a new, integrated, national police force. In December 1995, the Security Council further adjusted UNAMIR's mandate to focus primarily on facilitating the safe and voluntary return of refugees. UNAMIR's mandate came to an end on 3 March 1996. The withdrawal of the mission was complete in April 1996.

■ Operation "Turquoise"***

Duration: 22 June - 21 August 1994
Location: Rwanda
Command and Control HQ: Goma, Democratic Republic of the Congo
Commander: General Lafourcade
Authorization: S/RES/929 on 22 June 1994
Function: On 19 June 1994, Secretary-General Boutros Boutros-Ghali, in a letter

addressed to the President of the Security Council (S/1994/728), recommended that "with the failure of Member States to promptly provide the resources necessary for the implementation" of UNAMIR's expanded mandate as outlined in Security Council resolution 918 of 17 May 1994, the Council "may wish to consider the offer of the Government of France to undertake, subject to Security Council authorization, a French-commanded multinational operation in conjunction with other Member States, under Chapter VII of the Charter of the United Nations, to assure the security and protection of displaced persons and civilians at risk in Rwanda."

On 21 June 1994, the Permanent Representative of France to the United Nations wrote to the Secretary-General (S/1994/734) and stated, inter alia, the following:

"The humanitarian situation in Rwanda is an ongoing disaster. The cease-fire is not being respected by the parties, and massacres of civilians are continuing on a large scale.

"... Against that background, the Government of France and Senegal are prepared to send a force in without delay, so as to maintain a presence pending the arrival of the expanded UNAMIR. They are in contact with other Member States likely to join the operation. The objectives assigned to that force would be the same ones assigned to UNAMIR by the Security Council, i.e. contributing to the security and protection of displaced persons, refugees and civilians in danger in Rwanda, by means including the establishment and maintenance, where possible, of safe humanitarian areas. That objective naturally excludes any interference in the development of the balance of military

---

*** Although approved by the Security Council, Operation "Turquoise" was a multinational humanitarian operation, not a United Nations mission.

forces between the parties involved in the conflict.

"In the spirit of resolution 794 of 3 December 1992, our Governments would like, as a legal framework for their intervention, a resolution under Chapter VII of the Charter of the United Nations giving them a mandate to act until the expanded UNAMIR is deployed. As we see it, the interim force should be able to withdraw towards the middle of August at the latest, after handing over to UNAMIR when its reinforcements have been deployed."

In its resolution 929 adopted on 22 June 1994, the Security Council, after "determining that the magnitude of the humanitarian crisis in Rwanda constitutes a threat to peace and security in the region", and acting under Chapter VII of the Charter, authorized "the establishment of a temporary operation under national command and control aimed at contributing, in an impartial way, to the security and protection of displaced persons, refugees and civilians at risk in Rwanda", on the understanding that the costs of implementing the operation will be borne by the participating Member States.

The Council further decided that the operation will be limited to a period of two months, unless the Secretary-General determined that the expanded UNAMIR was still not able to carry out its mandate.

In accordance with the Security Council's request, France, on behalf of participating countries, submitted three reports to the Council on the implementation of the operation (see documents S/1994/795 of 5 July 1994, S/1994/933 of 4 August 1994, and S/1994/1100 of 27 September 1994). In the third and last report, France informed the Council that Operation "Turquoise", launched on 22 June 1994 upon the adoption of Security Council resolution 929, concluded its mission on 21 August 1994.

Central African countries affected by landmines	
Country	Estimated # of landmines
Angola	15,000,000
Burundi	N/A
Chad	70,000
Dem. Rep. of the Congo	N/A
Rwanda	250,000

Department of Humanitarian Affairs
30 October 1997

Persons of concern to UNHCR, at 1 January 1997, by category Region: Africa			
Refugees	Returnees	Internally displaced	Total
4,341,000	1,693,000	2,058,000	8,091,000

United Nations High Commissioner for Refugees

It is widely estimated that Angola has the largest number of landmines per capita in the world.

United Nations General Assembly Resolutions
dealing with the UN Standing Advisory Committee
on Security Questions in Central Africa

A/RES/46/37 B

The General Assembly,

Recalling the purposes and principles of the United Nations and its primary responsibility for the maintenance of international peace and security in accordance with its Charter,

Bearing in mind the guidelines for general and complete disarmament adopted at its tenth special session, the first special session devoted to disarmament,

Recalling also its resolutions 43/78 H and 43/85 of 7 December 1988, 44/21 of 15 November 1989 and 45/58 M of 4 December 1990,

Considering the importance and effectiveness of confidence-building measures taken at the initiative and with the participation of all States concerned and taking into account the specific characteristics of each region, in that they can contribute to regional disarmament and to international security, in accordance with the principles of the Charter of the United Nations,

Convinced that the resources released by disarmament, including regional disarmament, can be devoted to economic and social development and to the protection of the environment for the benefit of all peoples, in particular those of the developing countries,

Bearing in mind the final document adopted by the States members of the Economic Community of Central African States on confidence-building measures, security, disarmament and development in their subregion (A/46/307-S/22805, annex.), at the seminar-workshop held at Yaounde from 17 to 21 June 1991,

1. Supports and encourages efforts aimed at promoting confidence-building measures at regional and subregional levels in order to ease regional tensions and to further disarmament and non-proliferation measures at regional and subregional levels in Central Africa;

2. Welcomes the initiative taken by the States members of the Economic Community of Central African States with a view to developing confidence-building measures, disarmament and development in their subregion, by, in particular, the creation, under the auspices of the United Nations, of a standing advisory committee on security questions in Central Africa;

3. Thanks the Secretary-General for his contribution to the Yaounde seminar-workshop and requests him to continue providing assistance to the Central African States in implementing the recommendations and conclusions set forth in the final document of the seminar-workshop, by, in particular, establishing the standing advisory committee on security questions in Central Africa;

4. Also requests the Secretary-General to submit to the General Assembly at its forty-seventh session a report on the implementation of the present resolution;

5. Decides to include in the provisional agenda of its forty-seventh session an item entitled "Regional confidence-building measures".

65th plenary meeting
6 December 1991

A/RES/47/53 F

The General Assembly,

Recalling the purposes and principles of the United Nations and its primary responsibility for the maintenance of international peace and security in accordance with its Charter,

Bearing in mind the guidelines for general and complete disarmament adopted at its tenth special session, the first special session devoted to disarmament,

Recalling also its resolutions 43/78 H and 43/85 of 7 December 1988, 44/21 of 15 November 1989, 45/58 M of 4 December 1990 and 46/37 B of 6 December 1991,

Considering the importance and effectiveness of confidence-building measures taken at the initiative and with the participation of all States concerned and taking into account the specific characteristics of each region, in that they can contribute to regional disarmament and to international security, in accordance with the principles of the Charter of the United Nations,

Convinced that the resources released by disarmament, including regional disarmament, can be devoted to economic and social development and to the protection of the environment for the benefit of all peoples, in particular those of the developing countries,

Bearing in mind the establishment by the Secretary-General on 28 May 1992 of the Standing Advisory Committee on Security Questions in Central Africa, the purpose of which is to encourage arms limitation, disarmament, non-proliferation and development in the subregion,

Bearing in mind also the appointment by the Secretary-General of a permanent Secretary of the Standing Advisory Committee on Security Questions in Central Africa,

1. Takes note of the report of the Secretary-General on regional confidence-building measures (A/47/511), which deals chiefly with the organizational meeting of the Standing Advisory Committee on Security Questions in Central Africa, held at Yaounde from 27 to 31 July 1992 under the auspices of the United Nations;

2. Supports and encourages efforts aimed at promoting confidence-building measures at regional and subregional levels in order to ease regional tensions and to further disarmament and non-proliferation measures at regional and subregional levels in Central Africa;

3. Welcomes the programme of work including confidence-building measures adopted by the States members of the Economic Community of Central African States at the organizational meeting of the Standing Advisory Committee;

4. Requests the Secretary-General to continue to provide assistance to the Central African States in implementing the programme of work of the Standing Advisory Committee;

5. Also requests the Secretary-General to submit to the General Assembly at its forty-eighth session a report on the implementation of the present resolution;

6. Decides to include in the provisional agenda of its forty-eighth session the item entitled "Regional confidence-building measures".

88th plenary meeting
15 December 1992

A/RES/48/76 A

<u>The General Assembly</u>,

<u>Recalling</u> the purposes and principles of the United Nations and its primary responsibility for the maintenance of international peace and security in accordance with the Charter of the United Nations,

<u>Bearing in mind</u> the guidelines for general and complete disarmament adopted at its tenth special session, the first special session devoted to disarmament,

<u>Recalling also</u> its resolutions 43/78 H and 43/85 of 7 December 1988, 44/21 of 15 November 1989, 45/58 M of 4 December 1990, 46/37 B of 6 December 1991 and 47/53 F of 15 December 1992,

<u>Considering</u> the importance and effectiveness of confidence-building measures taken at the initiative and with the participation of all States concerned and taking into account the specific characteristics of each region, in that they can contribute to regional disarmament and to international security, in accordance with the principles of the Charter,

<u>Convinced</u> that the resources released by disarmament, including regional disarmament, can be devoted to economic and social development and to the protection of the environment for the benefit of all peoples, in particular those of the developing countries,

<u>Bearing in mind</u> the establishment by the Secretary-General on 28 May 1992 of the Standing Advisory Committee on Security Questions in Central Africa, the purpose of which is to encourage arms limitation, disarmament, non-proliferation and development in the subregion,

1. <u>Takes note</u> of the report of the Secretary-General on regional confidence-building measures (A/48/412), which deals chiefly with the meetings of the Standing Advisory Committee on Security Questions in Central Africa, held at Bujumbura in March 1993 and at Libreville in August and September 1993;

2. <u>Reaffirms</u> its support for efforts aimed at promoting confidence-building measures at the regional and subregional levels in order to ease regional tensions and to further disarmament, non-proliferation and the peaceful settlement of disputes in Central Africa;

3. <u>Also reaffirms</u> its support for the programme of work of the Standing Advisory Committee adopted at the organizational meeting of the Committee held at Yaoundé from 27 to 31 July 1992;

4. <u>Welcomes</u> the results of the meetings of the Standing Advisory Committee held at Bujumbura and at Libreville, particularly the adoption of the non-aggression pact between the States members of the Economic Community of Central African States, a pact that is likely to contribute to the prevention of conflicts and to confidence-building in the subregion;

5. <u>Takes note</u> of the readiness of the States members of the Economic Community of Central African States to reduce the military forces, equipment and budgets in the subregion and to carry out a study on that subject;

6. <u>Requests</u> the Secretary-General to continue to provide assistance to the Central African States in implementing the programme of work of the Standing Advisory Committee;

7. <u>Also requests</u> the Secretary-General to submit to the General Assembly at its forty-ninth session a report on the implementation of the present resolution;

8. Decides to include in the provisional agenda of its forty-ninth session the item entitled "Regional confidence-building measures".

81st plenary meeting
16 December 1993

A/RES/49/76 C

The General Assembly,

Recalling the purposes and principles of the United Nations and its primary responsibility for the maintenance of international peace and security in accordance with the Charter of the United Nations,

Bearing in mind the guidelines for general and complete disarmament adopted at its tenth special session, the first special session devoted to disarmament,

Recalling also its resolutions 43/78 H and 43/85 of 7 December 1988, 44/21 of 15 November 1989, 45/58 M of 4 December 1990, 46/37 B of 6 December 1991, 47/53 F of 15 December 1992 and 48/76 A of 16 December 1993,

Considering the importance and effectiveness of confidence-building measures taken at the initiative and with the participation of all States concerned and taking into account the specific characteristics of each region, in that they can contribute to regional disarmament and to international security, in accordance with the principles of the Charter,

Convinced that the resources released by disarmament, including regional disarmament, can be devoted to economic and social development and to the protection of the environment for the benefit of all peoples, in particular those of the developing countries,

Bearing in mind the establishment by the Secretary-General on 28 May 1992 of the Standing Advisory Committee on Security Questions in Central Africa, the purpose of which is to encourage arms limitation, disarmament, non-proliferation and development in the subregion,

1. Takes note of the report of the Secretary-General on regional confidence-building measures (A/49/546), which deals chiefly with the meetings of the Standing Advisory Committee on Security Questions in Central Africa, held at Yaoundé in April and September 1994;

2. Reaffirms its support for efforts aimed at promoting confidence-building measures at the regional and subregional levels in order to ease regional tensions and to further disarmament, non-proliferation and the peaceful settlement of disputes in Central Africa;

3. Also reaffirms its support for the programme of work of the Standing Advisory Committee adopted at the organizational meeting of the Committee held at Yaoundé from 27 to 31 July 1992;

4. Takes note of the readiness of the States members of the Economic Community of Central African States to reduce the military forces, equipment and budgets in the subregion and to continue reviewing the studies carried out on the subject with a view to reaching agreements to that end;

5. Welcomes with satisfaction the initialling of the Non-Aggression Pact between the States members of the Economic Community of Central African States, which is likely to contribute to the prevention of conflicts and to confidence-building in the subregion, and encourages those States to sign the Pact as soon as possible;

6. **Also welcomes with satisfaction** the decision taken by the States members of the Economic Community of Central African States to participate in peace-keeping operations of the United Nations and the Organization of African Unity and, to that end, to establish units specializing in peace-keeping operations within their respective armed forces;

7. **Requests** Member States and non-governmental organizations to assist and to promote the training and preparation of units specializing in peace operations in the member countries of the Standing Advisory Committee;

8. **Requests** the Secretary-General to continue to provide assistance to the Central African States in implementing the programme of work of the Standing Advisory Committee;

9. **Also requests** the Secretary-General to submit to the General Assembly at its fiftieth session a report on the implementation of the present resolution;

10. **Decides** to include in the provisional agenda of its fiftieth session the item entitled "Regional confidence-building measures".

90th plenary meeting
15 December 1994

A/RES/50/71 B

The General Assembly,

Recalling the purposes and principles of the United Nations and its primary responsibility for the maintenance of international peace and security in accordance with the Charter of the United Nations,

Bearing in mind the guidelines for general and complete disarmament adopted at its tenth special session, the first special session devoted to disarmament,

Recalling its resolutions 43/78 H and 43/85 of 7 December 1988, 44/21 of 15 November 1989, 45/58 M of 4 December 1990, 46/37 B of 6 December 1991, 47/53 F of 15 December 1992, 48/76 A of 16 December 1993 and 49/76 C of 15 December 1994,

Considering the importance and effectiveness of confidence-building measures taken at the initiative and with the participation of all States concerned and taking into account the specific characteristics of each region, in that they can contribute to regional disarmament and to international security, in accordance with the principles of the Charter,

Convinced that the resources released by disarmament, including regional disarmament, can be devoted to economic and social development and to the protection of the environment for the benefit of all peoples, in particular those of the developing countries,

Bearing in mind the establishment by the Secretary-General on 28 May 1992 of the Standing Advisory Committee on Security Questions in Central Africa, the purpose of which is to encourage arms limitation, disarmament, non-proliferation and development in the subregion,

1. **Takes note** of the report of the Secretary-General on regional confidence-building measures (A/50/474), which deals with the sixth and seventh meetings of the Standing Advisory Committee on Security Questions in Central Africa, held at Brazzaville in March and August 1995;

2. **Reaffirms its support** for efforts aimed at promoting confidence-building measures at regional and subregional levels in order to ease tensions and conflicts in the subregion

and to further disarmament, non-proliferation and the peaceful settlement of disputes in Central Africa;

3. Also reaffirms its support for the programme of work of the Standing Advisory Committee adopted at the organizational meeting of the Committee held at Yaoundé in July 1992;

4. Takes note of the Brazzaville Declaration on Cooperation for Peace and Security in Central Africa (A/50/474, annex I) and urges the States members of the Standing Advisory Committee to implement it promptly;

5. Notes the readiness of the States members of the Standing Advisory Committee to reduce the military forces, equipment and budgets in the subregion and to continue reviewing the studies carried out on the subject with a view to reaching agreements to that end;

6. Welcomes the initialling of the Non-Aggression Pact between the States members of the Standing Advisory Committee, which is likely to contribute to the prevention of conflicts and to confidence-building in the subregion, and encourages those States to sign the Pact as soon as possible;

7. Welcomes with satisfaction the decision by the States members of the Standing Advisory Committee to participate in peace operations of the United Nations and the Organization of African Unity and, to that end, to establish units specializing in peace operations within their respective armed forces;

8. Also welcomes with satisfaction the participation of some of the States members of the Standing Advisory Committee in the peace operations deployed in the subregion;

9. Requests Member States and governmental and non-governmental

organizations to promote and to facilitate the holding of a training programme on peace operations in the subregion with a view to strengthening the capacity of the units specializing in peace operations in the armed forces of the States members of the Standing Advisory Committee;

10. Requests the Secretary-General to continue to provide assistance to the States members of the Standing Advisory Committee and to establish a trust fund to which Member States and governmental and non-governmental organizations may make additional voluntary contributions for the implementation of the programme of work of the Committee;

11. Also requests the Secretary-General to submit to the General Assembly at its fifty-first session a report on the implementation of the present resolution;

12. Decides to include in the provisional agenda of its fifty-first session the item entitled "Regional confidence-building measures".

90th plenary meeting
12 December 1995

A/RES/51/46 C

The General Assembly,

Recalling the purposes and principles of the United Nations and its primary responsibility for the maintenance of international peace and security in accordance with the Charter of the United Nations,

Bearing in mind the guidelines for general and complete disarmament adopted at its tenth special session, the first special session devoted to disarmament,

Recalling its resolutions 43/78 H and

43/85 of 7 December 1988, 44/21 of 15 November 1989, 45/58 M of 4 December 1990, 46/37 B of 6 December 1991, 47/53 F of 15 December 1992, 48/76 A of 16 December 1993, 49/76 C of 15 December 1994 and 50/71 B of 12 December 1995,

Considering the importance and effectiveness of confidence-building measures taken at the initiative and with the participation of all States concerned and taking into account the specific characteristics of each region, in that they can contribute to regional disarmament and to international security, in accordance with the principles of the Charter,

Convinced that the resources released by disarmament, including regional disarmament, can be devoted to economic and social development and to the protection of the environment for the benefit of all peoples, in particular those of the developing countries,

Convinced also that development can be achieved only in a climate of peace, security and mutual confidence both within and among States,

Bearing in mind the establishment by the Secretary-General on 28 May 1992 of the United Nations Standing Advisory Committee on Security Questions in Central Africa, the purpose of which is to encourage arms limitation, disarmament, non-proliferation and development in the subregion,

Recalling the Brazzaville Declaration on Cooperation for Peace and Security in Central Africa (A/50/474, annex I),

1. Takes note of the report of the Secretary-General on regional confidence-building measures (A/51/287), which deals with the activities of the United Nations Standing Advisory Committee on Security Questions in Central Africa in the period since the adoption by the General Assembly

of resolution 50/71 B;

2. Reaffirms its support for efforts aimed at promoting confidence-building measures at regional and subregional levels in order to ease tensions and conflicts in the subregion and to further disarmament, non-proliferation and the peaceful settlement of disputes in Central Africa;

3. Also reaffirms its support for the programme of work of the Standing Advisory Committee adopted at the organizational meeting of the Committee held at Yaoundé in July 1992;

4. Welcomes the fact that the Committee's programme of work has led to specific actions and measures promoting confidence-building and security in the Central African subregion;

5. Notes the holding of the First Summit of Heads of State and Government of Countries Members of the United Nations Standing Advisory Committee on Security Questions in Central Africa, at Yaoundé on 8 July 1996;

6. Welcomes with great satisfaction the signature at that Summit of the Non-Aggression Pact between the States members of the United Nations Standing Advisory Committee, and reaffirms its conviction that the Pact is likely to contribute to the prevention of conflicts and further confidence-building in the Central African subregion;

7. Invites the States members of the Standing Advisory Committee that have not yet signed the Pact to do so, and encourages all member States to expedite ratification so that it may enter into force as soon as possible;

8. Welcomes with satisfaction the Final Declaration of the First Summit of the Standing Advisory Committee (A/51/274-S/1996/631, annex) which aims at the

implementation of the following measures:

(a) The promotion of participatory systems of governance as a means of preventing conflicts;

(b) The organization, under United Nations auspices, of training seminars for officers in the armed forces, republican guard, gendarmerie and police forces of the Central African States, in order to promote a culture of peace by explaining, once again, their role in a democratic context;

(c) The development of a programme to combat illicit arms trafficking, in order to remove this source of insecurity and a threat to the stability of States in the subregion;

(d) The setting-up, under United Nations auspices, of an early warning system as the basic instrument for preventive diplomacy in Central Africa;

(e) The strengthening of cooperation between States of the subregion and bilateral and multilateral partners on the question of peace and security in Central Africa;

9. Expresses its conviction that the democratic process offers a valuable means to build confidence, promote development and prevent conflicts, and welcomes with satisfaction the decision taken by the States members of the Standing Advisory Committee to hold a subregional conference at Brazzaville in January 1997 on the topic "Democratic institutions and peace in Central Africa";

10. Welcomes the holding, under United Nations auspices, of the first training seminar for instructors in peace operations, at Yaoundé from 9 to 17 September 1996, with a view to strengthening the capacity of the units specializing in peace operations in the armed forces of the States members of the Standing Advisory Committee;

11. Expresses its gratitude to those Governments which responded favourably to the request from the General Assembly and contributed towards financing the aforementioned training seminar;

12. Emphasizes once again the importance of continuing with this training programme in order to strengthen the participation of States members of the Standing Advisory Committee in future United Nations peace operations;

13. Commends the Secretary-General for having established the Trust Fund for the United Nations Standing Advisory Committee on Security Questions in Central Africa;

14. Appeals to Member States and governmental and non-governmental organizations to make additional voluntary contributions to the Trust Fund for the implementation of the programme of work of the Standing Advisory Committee, in particular the measures and objectives referred to in paragraphs 8, 9 and 12 of the present resolution;

15. Requests the Secretary-General to continue to provide assistance to the States members of the Standing Advisory Committee to ensure that they are able to carry on with their efforts;

16. Also requests the Secretary-General to submit to the General Assembly at its fifty-second session a report on the implementation of the present resolution;

17. Decides to include in the provisional agenda of its fifty-second session the item entitled "Regional confidence-building measures".

79th plenary meeting
10 December 1996

Reports of the Secretary-General
*dealing with the UN Standing Advisory Committee
on Security Questions in Central Africa*

A/47/511

I. INTRODUCTION

1. At its forty-sixth session, on 6 December 1991, the General Assembly adopted resolution 46/37 B, which contains the following key paragraphs:

"The General Assembly,

"...

"1. Supports and encourages efforts aimed at promoting confidence-building measures at the regional and subregional levels in order to ease regional tensions and to further disarmament and non-proliferation measures at the regional and subregional levels in Central Africa;

"2. Welcomes the initiative taken by the States members of the Economic Community of Central African States with a view to developing confidence-building measures, disarmament and development in their subregion, by, in particular, the creation, under the auspices of the United Nations, of a standing advisory committee on security questions in Central Africa;

"3. Thanks the Secretary-General for his contribution to the Yaounde seminar-workshop and requests him to continue providing assistance to the Central African States in implementing the recommend-ations and conclusions set forth in the final document of the seminar-workshop, by, in particular, establishing the standing advisory committee on security questions in Central Africa;

"4. Also requests the Secretary-General

to submit to the General Assembly at its forty-seventh session a report on the implementation of the present resolution;

"5. Decides to include in the provisional agenda of its forty-seventh session an item entitled 'Regional confidence-building measures'."

2. This report is submitted by the Secretary-General in implementation of paragraph 4 of the resolution.

II. ORGANIZATIONAL MEETING OF THE STANDING ADVISORY COMMITTEE

3. In accordance with the provisions of paragraph 3 of General Assembly resolution 46/37 B, on 28 May 1992 the Secretary-General established the Standing Advisory Committee on Security Questions in Central Africa under the auspices of the United Nations. The purpose of the Committee is to develop confidence-building measures and to encourage arms limitation and development in the Central African subregion. The Committee's deliberations will take place at different levels, including meetings of experts (high-level military and civilian officials), ministerial meetings and talks between the heads of State concerned at their annual meetings in the context of the Economic Community of Central African States (ECCAS). The Secretary-General appointed Mr. Sammy Kum Buo of the Secretariat's Office for Disarmament Affairs (Department of Political Affairs) as Secretary of the Standing Advisory Committee.

4. The Committee held its ministerial-level organizational meeting at Yaounde from 27 to 31 July 1992 with the assistance provided

by the Office for Disarmament Affairs from extra-budgetary funding. The Director of the Office represented the Secretary-General at the meeting. Delegations from the following countries attended the meeting: Burundi, Cameroon, Central African Republic, Chad, Congo, Equatorial Guinea, Gabon, Rwanda, Sao Tome and Principe and Zaire.[1] Most of the delegations were headed by the minister for foreign affairs or the minister of defence of the country concerned.

5. During the opening ceremony, presided over by Mr. Jacques-Roger Booh Booh, Minister for Foreign Affairs of the Republic of Cameroon, Burundi's Secretary of State for Cooperation and head of delegation, Mr. Charles Itangishaka, read a message from Mr. Pierre Buyoya, President of the Republic of Burundi and current President of ECCAS, underlining the importance of confidence-building measures for the stability and development of the subregion.

6. The officers of the Committee were elected by consensus as follows: Chairman, Cameroon; First Vice-Chairman, Gabon; Second Vice-Chairman, Burundi; General Rapporteur, Sao Tome and Principe.

7. The Committee adopted the following procedural decisions:

(a) The Committee's rules of procedure shall be those of the General Assembly;

(b) The officers of the Committee shall serve for a term of six months and the offices shall be held by rotation;

(c) The Committee gave its Chairman a mandate to hold consultations with a view to inviting a number of interested States and organizations to participate in its work as observers;

---

[1] Angola, which was recently admitted as a full member of ECCAS, was unable to attend this meeting.

(d) Given the importance of the role of political will in promoting confidence-building and security measures, the Committee requested the head of the delegation of Burundi to transmit to the head of State of Burundi in his capacity as current President of ECCAS, its wish to have issues relating to confidence-building and security put on the agenda of the annual summit meeting of ECCAS heads of State.

8. At the organizational meeting, whose purpose was to draw up the Committee's programme and calendar of work, two keynote presentations were made. The first, entitled "Promotion of confidence-building and security measures in the Central African subregion", was made by Gen. Idriss Ngari, Chief of Staff of the Gabonese Armed Forces and President of the 1988 ECCAS Conference on the Promotion of Confidence, Security and Development. The second presentation, entitled "Public affairs management and development: Priorities for Central Africa", was given by Mr. Emmanuel E. Mbi, World Bank senior administrator for Africa. In addition, the Republic of Cameroon submitted a working paper entitled "Standing Advisory Committee on Questions of Security in Central Africa: Proposals by Cameroon".

9. After a thorough exchange of views among participants, and taking into account General Assembly resolution 46/37 B and the statements made and papers submitted at the organizational meeting, the Committee adopted the programme of work set out below, which divides the topics to be considered into two groups of proposals according to the Committee's calendar of work.

III. PROGRAMME OF WORK OF THE COMMITTEE

10.   Classification of confidence-building and security measures according to priority:

Priority I. Measures that could be implemented during the initial stage of activities

A. Preventive diplomacy

1. Respect for the sovereignty of States.

2. Adherence by all States of the subregion to international legal instruments on arms limitation and disarmament.

3. Encouragement and promotion of the policy of voluntary repatriation of refugees and application of practical measures to enable them to reintegrate into society, as a humanitarian element of confidence-building.

4. Conclusion of a subregional non-aggression pact.

5. Establishment of hotlines between heads of State of the subregion.

6. Increased meetings of heads of State of the subregion.

7. Organization of regular joint meetings of ministers of defence, of the interior and for foreign affairs, as well as of chiefs of staff of the subregion.

8. Establishment and improvement of transparency in military activities: prior notification to other States of each State's military manoeuvres, and invitation of observers of the countries concerned.

9. Environmental safeguards.

10. Agreement on the part of all States in the subregion not to produce, acquire or transfer weapons of mass destruction, such as nuclear, chemical and biological weapons.

B. Peace building

1. Strengthening and consolidation of the democratization process and promotion of respect for human rights in the subregion.

2. Respect for commitments undertaken between States of the subregion.

3. Establishment of a crisis-management body in each member State.

4. Increased involvement of the people and the media in the pursuit of the ideals of peace, security and development in the subregion.

5. Measures to promote awareness among potential emigrants or immigrants of the laws and the culture of receiving countries.

6. Increased cooperation in the area of emigration and immigration through the drafting or implementation of subregional legislation on the movement of persons.

7. Expansion of cooperation and exchange programmes in the fields of information, culture and education.

8. Exchange of military delegations.

9. Elaboration of specific measures for promoting agreement on a balanced and gradual reduction of the military forces, equipment and budgets of the States of the subregion.

10. Assistance in connection with the restructuring of armies and redeployment of the military.

C. Peacemaking and peace-keeping

Establishment of a standing inter-State general staff for crisis management that might study the advisability of setting up a peace-keeping force, and ways of funding it.

D. Training of peace-keeping personnel

Development of cooperation with training institutions specializing in the field of conflict prevention and the management of peace-keeping operations.

E. Compliance and verification

Establishment of appropriate verification measures in conjunction with the confidence-building and security measures mentioned above.

Priority II. Measures that could be implemented at a later date

A. Preventive diplomacy

1. Expansion of each State's actual diplomatic presence in all the other countries of the subregion.

2. Strengthening of subregional cooperation in the field of military training.

3. Organization of joint military manoeuvres and exercises and mixed patrols.

4. Training, at the subregional level, in the management of emergency humanitarian assistance operations.

B. Peace building

I. Elaboration and strengthening of machinery and instruments for promoting efforts to settle disputes peacefully.

2. Strengthening of regional integration.

3. Development of cooperation between neighbouring countries through the creation of markets in border zones, expansion of contacts between border authorities and implementation of joint economic development projects in border zones.

4. Development of means of transport and communication between States of the subregion.

5. Creation of demilitarized zones and zones of peace.

C. Peacemaking and peace-keeping

Establishment of a standing inter-State general staff for crisis management that might study the advisability of setting up a peace-keeping force, and ways of funding it.

D. Training of peace-keeping personnel

Establishment of a subregional centre for the training of peace-keeping personnel.

E. Compliance and verification

Establishment of appropriate verification measures in conjunction with the confidence-building and security measures mentioned above.

IV. CONCLUSIONS

11. The discussions held during the organizational meeting of the Standing Advisory Committee on Security Questions in Central Africa, as well as the programme of work adopted at that meeting, have paved the way for effective collaboration between the United Nations and the member States of ECCAS to promote and consolidate peace and progress in the Central African subregion.

12. The General Assembly, in its resolution 46/37 B, expressed its support and encouragement for efforts of the Central African States aimed at promoting confidence-building measures in their area, and requested the Secretary-General to continue providing assistance in such efforts. The establishment of the Standing Advisory Committee is a first step in that direction. It will be very important to take advantage of the momentum generated by the establishment and inauguration of the

Committee so as to enable it to begin its substantive work, i.e., the drafting, adoption and implementation of specific confidence-building measures. The programme and calendar of work adopted at the organizational meeting of the Committee provide a useful starting-point for planning and implementing a rational and realistic strategy to coordinate United Nations support for this initiative.

13. The agreement on the part of the States of the Central African subregion to renounce the use of force as a political option in their relations, and instead to seek constructive and practical measures for strengthening trust and cooperation between States, represents a significant political change which deserves the full support and encouragement of the entire international community. If this initiative is successful, in addition to directly benefitting the nearly 100 million people who live in the subregion it will serve as a positive example for the rest of the subregion and even further afield, thus enhancing the prospects for carrying out a viable global peace programme.

A/48/412

I. INTRODUCTION

1. At its forty-seventh session, on 15 December 1992, the General Assembly adopted resolution 47/53 F, which contains the following key paragraphs:

"The General Assembly,

"...

"1. Takes note of the report of the Secretary-General on regional confidence-building measures, (A/47/511) which deals chiefly with the organizational meeting of the Standing Advisory Committee on Security Questions in Central Africa, held at Yaoundé from 27 to 31 July 1992 under the auspices of the United Nations;

"2. Supports and encourages efforts aimed at promoting confidence-building measures at regional and subregional levels in order to ease regional tensions and to further disarmament and non-proliferation measures at regional and subregional levels in Central Africa;

"3. Welcomes the programme of work including confidence-building measures adopted by the States members of the Economic Community of Central African States at the organizational meeting of the Standing Advisory Committee;

"4. Requests the Secretary-General to continue to provide assistance to the Central African States in implementing the programme of work of the Standing Advisory Committee;

"5. Also requests the Secretary-General to submit to the General Assembly at its forty-eighth session a report on the implementation of the present resolution;

"6. Decides to include in the provisional agenda of its forty-eighth session the item entitled 'Regional confidence-building measures'."

2. This report is submitted by the Secretary-General in implementation of paragraph 5 of the resolution.

3. The activities of the Standing Advisory Committee on Security Questions in Central Africa since the previous report of the Secretary-General mentioned above have been principally concerned with two important meetings on the implementation of the programme of work of the Committee.

II. SECOND MEETING OF THE STANDING ADVISORY COMMITTEE ON SECURITY QUESTIONS IN CENTRAL AFRICA

4. In accordance with the procedural decisions adopted at the meeting held at Yaoundé from 27 to 31 July 1992, the Standing Advisory Committee on Security Questions in Central Africa was held at Bujumbura at the expert level from 8 to 10 March 1993 and at the ministerial level from 11 to 12 March 1993.

5. Delegations from the following countries took part in the meeting: Burundi, Cameroon, Central African Republic, Chad, Congo, Equatorial Guinea, Gabon, Rwanda and Sao Tome and Principe. Zaire and Angola were unable to attend the meeting. The secretariat of the Economic Community of Central African States (ECCAS), which had been invited, was also unable to attend.

6. At the opening ceremony of the ministerial meeting, statements were made by the Acting Director of the United Nations Regional Centre for Peace and Disarmament in Africa, representative of the Director of the Office for Disarmament Affairs; Mr. Martin-Fidèle Magnaga, Minister of Defence, Security and Immigration of Gabon, First Vice-Chairman of the Committee, standing in for the Minister for Foreign Affairs of Cameroon, current Chairman of the Committee, unable to attend; and Mr. Libère Bararunyeretse, Minister for Foreign Affairs and Cooperation of Burundi and representative of the host country.

A. Election of officers

7. The officers of the Committee were elected by consensus, as follows: Chairman, Burundi; First Vice-Chairman, Gabon; Second Vice-Chairman, Congo; Rapporteur, Chad.

B. Progress of work

8. The participants in the meeting considered the following items:

1. Review of the status of international legal instruments concerning arms limitation and disarmament as they affect the States members of the Economic Community of Central African States

9. The Committee recommended that the States members of ECCAS should accede to multilateral disarmament agreements, and that the above-mentioned agenda item should be included in the agenda of the next meeting of the Standing Advisory Committee for updating.

2. Review of the geopolitical and security situation in the Central African subregion

10. In their exchange of views, the participants noted that the subregion was still faced with threats and suffered from various weaknesses and internal crises, the causes of which were internal and/or external.

11. After a brief consideration of the geopolitical and security situation in the subregion, the Committee made, inter alia, the following observations:

(a) The accumulation of weapons of mass destruction in the world remains, in global terms, a source of threat to peace and security in the subregion.

(b) The Central African subregion contains a number of specific threats which are liable to compromise peace and security within the region, in particular:

(i) Border problems;

(ii) The aggravation of socio-ethnic and socio-political rivalries;

(iii) The problem of refugees and displaced persons;

(iv) Natural disasters;

(v) Socio-economic problems;

(vi) The interplay of power and conflicts between States;

(vii) Arms transfers;

(viii) The North-South divide;

(ix) Traffic in drugs and narcotics;

(x) International terrorism.

12. Desiring to promote a climate of peace and security in the subregion, the ministerial meeting recommended that the member States of the subregion should implement the measures contained in the programme of work of the Standing Advisory Committee adopted in July 1992 at Yaoundé, and in particular that they should:

(a) Respect the rights of minorities;

(b) Create stable socio-economic and political conditions with a view to settling populations;

(c) Promote internal transparency in the management of democracy;

(d) Respect human rights;

(e) Draw up legal instruments for collective security;

(f) Respect bilateral and multilateral agreements.

13. Furthermore, the Committee recommended that review of the geopolitical and security situation in the subregion should be a permanent item on the agenda of its meetings and should be given priority consideration.

3. Consideration of the draft non-aggression pact between the States members of ECCAS

14. After considering the preliminary draft of the non-aggression pact between the States members of ECCAS, the Committee decided to submit the resulting draft text to the member States for consideration and adoption at the next meeting of the Committee.

4. Elaboration of specific measures for promoting the establishment of a standing inter-State general staff for crisis management with a view to setting up a subregional peace-keeping force

15. After a concerted analysis of this item, measures of a political, legal and structural nature were considered and it was agreed that they should be examined in greater depth at the next meeting of the Committee.

16. In anticipation of the establishment of a subregional collective security management mechanism, the Committee recommended that the functional relations between ECCAS, the Organization of African Unity (OAU), the United Nations and any other partner should be taken into account.

17. With that prospect in mind, the Committee proposed that the implementation of those measures should be in keeping with the collective security management mechanisms being prepared by OAU.

5. Elaboration of specific measures for promoting agreement on a balanced and gradual reduction of the military forces, equipment and budgets of member States

18. In view of the complexity of the question, the participants recommended that a study should be undertaken on the restructuring of the armies and reconversion of military personnel, which would serve as a working document for further discussions.

19. The Committee requested the assistance of the United Nations for the undertaking of that study.

6. Other matters

20. Having noted the current financial difficulties facing the ECCAS secretariat, and in view of the necessary involvement of that organization in the process of maintaining peace and security in the subregion, the Committee proposed that the costs incurred by the Secretary-General of ECCAS or his representative when attending meetings of the Committee should be borne by the host country.

III. THIRD MEETING OF THE STANDING ADVISORY COMMITTEE ON SECURITY QUESTIONS IN CENTRAL AFRICA

21. The third meeting of the Standing Advisory Committee on Security Questions in Central Africa was held at Libreville at the expert level from 30 August to 1 September 1993 and at the ministerial level from 2 to 3 September 1993.

22. Delegations from all countries represented on the Committee took part in the meeting: Angola, Burundi, Cameroon, Central African Republic, Chad, Congo, Equatorial Guinea, Gabon, Rwanda, Sao Tome and Principe and Zaire.

23. At the opening ceremony of the ministerial meeting, statements were made by His Excellency Mr. Martin-Fidèle Magnaga, Minister of National Defence, Security and Immigration, representative of the host Government, and Ambassador Hassen Fodha, representative of the Secretary-General of the United Nations. His Excellency Mr. Sylvestre Ntibantunganya, Minister for Foreign Affairs and Cooperation of Burundi, current Chairman of the Committee, delivered the opening address.

A. Election of officers

24. The officers of the Committee were elected by consensus, as follows: Chairman: Gabon; First Vice-Chairman: Congo; Second Vice-Chairman: Angola; Rapporteur: Zaire.

B. Progress of work

25. The participants in the meeting considered the following items:

(a) Review of the status of international legal instruments concerning arms limitation and disarmament as they affect the countries of the subregion;

(b) Review of the geopolitical and security situation in the Central African subregion;

(c) Exchange of views on the theme "Democratization, human rights and stability in Central Africa";

(d) Elaboration of specific measures for promoting agreement on a balanced and gradual reduction of the military forces, equipment and budgets of member States;

(e) Elaboration of measures for promoting the establishment of a standing inter-State general staff for crisis management with a view to setting up a subregional peace-keeping force;

(f) Consideration of the draft non-aggression pact between the States members of ECCAS.

1. Review of the status of international legal instruments concerning arms limitation and disarmament as they affect the countries of the subregion

26. Having considered the matter, the Committee emphasized that it was in the interest of all the States of the subregion to accede to international legal instruments

concerning arms limitation and disarmament and invited them to sign and/or ratify the instruments within 18 months, with due regard for the constitutional procedures appropriate to each country.

2. Review of the geopolitical and security situation in the Central African subregion

27. Following an exchange of views on this matter and having regard to the crises and armed conflicts noted in certain countries of the subregion, the Committee recommended that its officers should:

  (a) Play a more committed political role in the search for solutions to crises and conflicts that potentially threaten the peace, stability and development of a member country of the subregion;

  (b) Initiate and join in any action tending to promote a peaceful solution to crises and conflicts in the subregion; and

  (c) Undertake solidarity missions to States which request them, in order to express to the peoples of these sister countries the support and active solidarity of member countries.

28. The Committee also urged member countries to participate in observer missions and peace-keeping and humanitarian operations, under the auspices of the United Nations and/or OAU, in subregional conflict areas.

29. With regard to the situation in Rwanda, the Committee welcomed the signature of the Arusha Peace Agreement of 4 August 1993, which opened up the prospect of an era of peace and national reconciliation in that country. It urged the international community to support the effective implementation of the Agreement.

30. The Committee recommended that member States of the subregion should show their active solidarity with the peace process unfolding in that sister country and use their influence at the United Nations to encourage it to proceed as soon as possible to the deployment of the neutral international force provided for in the Peace Agreement.

31. As for the situation in Angola, the Committee expressed its concern with regard to the delay in the peace process in that country. It urged its Angolan brothers to follow the path of negotiation in preference to armed struggle in the interest of their people.

32. The Committee supported and encouraged all the efforts made at both the bilateral and the multilateral level to find a negotiated solution to the Angolan conflict.

33. Stressing the importance of the Declaration of the OAU Heads of State and Government on the situation in Angola (AHG/Decl.2-XXIX), the Committee urgently requested UNITA to comply with Security Council resolution 851 (1993).

34. Lastly, given the security problems that can arise as a result of emigration and immigration in the subregion, the Committee recommended that a group of experts should be appointed to draw up subregional legislation on the movement of persons.

35. The Committee also recommended that the questions of emigration and immigration in the subregion should be included in the agenda of its next meeting.

3. Exchange of views on the theme "Democratization, human rights and stability in Africa"

36. Following an extensive exchange of views, preceded by an introductory statement on the issue by Professor Isaac Nguema, former Chairman of the African Commission on Human and Peoples' Rights, the Committee encouraged the States of the subregion to pursue and

strengthen the democratization process in their respective countries, at the same time respecting and promoting human rights, in order to ensure the peace, stability and development of the subregion.

37. The Committee also invited all those involved in politics to further the democratic process through consultation, dialogue and negotiation in the higher interests of their nation.

4. Elaboration of specific measures for promoting agreement on a balanced and gradual reduction of the military forces, equipment and budgets of member States

38. Having considered this question, the Committee reiterated its recommendation that the United Nations should be asked to carry out a study of the issue, in collaboration with the countries of the subregion. The study should take into account the particular situations in the various countries of the subregion and the specific missions which should be assigned to the armed forces in the field of development.

39. The Committee declared that it supported the United Nations position on disarmament and invited member States to provide the necessary information to the United Nations Register of Conventional Arms.

5. Elaboration of measures for promoting the establishment of a standing inter-State general staff for crisis management with a view to setting up a subregional peace-keeping force

40. After consideration of this item, beginning with an introductory statement by Ambassador Olara Otunnu, President of the International Peace Academy, the Committee recommended that its investigation should continue until the next session and that each member State should make its views known.

41. Until such time as a system to manage crises and conflicts in the subregion should be set up, however, the Committee recommended the adoption of the following transitional measures relating to policy, legislation and administration:

(1) Policy measures

42. In view of the relation between security and development, the Committee recommends the following:

(a) ECCAS should resume participation in the process of economic integration, taking into account the security of the subregion;

(b) All the organizations concerned with the economic integration of the subregion - ECCAS, the Central African Customs and Economic Union (CACEU) and the Economic Community of the Great Lakes Countries (CEPGL) - should be invited to its meetings;

(c) A national body for the management of crises and conflicts should be set up in each member State;

(d) Member States should be encouraged to intensify their bilateral cooperation initiatives in the field of subregional security.

(2) Legal measures

(a) A protocol should be added to the treaty establishing ECCAS, granting it powers in the field of security;

(b) A draft protocol of mutual assistance should be drawn up to provide the essential legal framework for the creation of a joint general staff for the management of crises and conflicts, as well as a subregional peace-keeping force;

(c) A study of the typology of crises and conflicts in the subregion should be carried out.

(3) Administrative measures

(a) A temporary general staff committee for the subregion should be set up;

(b) Military attachés should be sent to the diplomatic missions of ECCAS member States;

(c) Within the armed forces of each member State a unit specializing in peace-keeping missions should be established;

(d) A training programme for peace missions in the subregion should be organized in collaboration with the United Nations;

(e) Study visits should be organized for military or police delegations to other countries in the subregion, with a view to perpetuating and strengthening the existing relationship between officers of different countries.

6. Consideration of the draft non-aggression pact

43. After due consideration the Committee decided to adopt the draft non-aggression pact and to submit it for signature by the Heads of State and/or Government of the subregion.

IV. CONCLUSION

44. The Committee's second and third meetings, held in 1993, represented a major step towards the fulfilment of the Committee's programme of work adopted in July 1992. All the member countries of the Committee were committed to a pragmatic and realistic approach to the Committee's work, which was both important and delicate. Such commitment is more than ever essential at a time when conflicts and other threats to security are exacerbating economic difficulties and seriously

jeopardizing the well-being of the peoples of the subregion. For this reason the Committee is duty bound to show itself to be a harbinger of hope in the search for ways and means to achieve the peaceful settlement of disputes between States of the Central African subregion.

45. The adoption of the non-aggression pact between the countries of the subregion and the Committee's decision to mandate its officers to play a more active political role and to undertake visits of solidarity and sympathy to countries engaged in conflict, among other initiatives, mark the beginning of major achievements in the field of preventive diplomacy and confidence-building, which have already shifted the Committee's work into higher gear after only a year of existence. The readiness of the member countries of the Committee and of the international community to provide the resources needed to facilitate this revitalized role of the officers will surely enable the Committee to achieve its noble and pressing objectives.

A/49/546

I. INTRODUCTION

1. At its forty-eighth session, the General Assembly, in resolution 48/76 A of 16 December 1993, welcomed the results of the meetings of the Standing Advisory Committee held at Bujumbura and at Libreville, particularly the adoption of the non-aggression pact between the States members of the Economic Community of Central Africa States, a pact likely to contribute to the prevention of conflicts and to confidence-building in the subregion. It requested the Secretary-General to continue to provide assistance to the Central African States in implementing the programme of work of the Standing Advisory Committee, and it also requested the Secretary-General to submit to the Assembly at its forty-ninth

session a report on the implementation of the resolution.

2. The present report is submitted by the Secretary-General in implementation of that resolution.

II. FOURTH MEETING OF THE STANDING ADVISORY COMMITTEE ON SECURITY QUESTIONS IN CENTRAL AFRICA

3. The fourth meeting of the Standing Advisory Committee on Security Questions in Central Africa was held at Yaoundé, from 4 to 6 April 1994 at the expert level and on 7 and 8 April 1994 at the ministerial level.

4. Delegations from 11 States members of the Committee took part in the meeting: Angola, Burundi, Cameroon, Central African Republic, Chad, Congo, Equatorial Guinea, Gabon, Rwanda, Sao Tome and Principe, and Zaire.

5. At the opening ceremony of the ministerial meeting, statements were made by Mr. Ferdinand Léopold Oyono, Minister for Foreign Affairs of Cameroon; Mr. Sammy Kum Buo, Secretary of the Committee; Mr. Herbert McLeod, Resident Coordinator of United Nations Operations in Eritrea, representative of the United Nations Secretary-General; and General Idriss Ngari, Minister of Defence and Immigration of Gabon, current Chairman of the Committee.

A. Election of officers

6. The officers of the Committee were elected by consensus, as follows: Chairman: Cameroon; First Vice-Chairman: Congo; Second Vice-Chairman: Angola; and Rapporteur: Zaire.

B. Progress of work

1. Review of the geopolitical and security situation in the Central African subregion

7. In its exchange of views, the Committee noted that crises and conflicts which were the products of ethnic rivalry, initiation into democracy and border disputes persisted in a number of countries, including Angola, Burundi, Rwanda and Cameroon.

8. At the same time, it welcomed the truces and the first signs of a climate of peace that would enable the process of democratization and economic progress to resume and be strengthened, especially in Chad, the Congo, Gabon and Zaire.

9. Given the above situation, the Committee made the following recommendations:

Angola

10. The Committee reiterated its concern at the delay in the peace process in Angola and once again urged its Angolan brothers to take advantage of the current talks at Lusaka to reach a just and equitable solution conducive to the restoration of peace in their country.

11. The Committee expressed support and encouragement for all the efforts by the Government of Angola, at the national, bilateral and multilateral levels, to find a negotiated solution to the conflict.

12. The Committee recommended that its officers dispatch a mission to Angola to inform the fraternal Angolan people of the active solidarity of the member States.

13. While again emphasizing the importance of the Declaration on the situation in Angola (AHG/Decl.2 (XXIX)) adopted by the Conference of Heads of State and Government of the Organization of African Unity (OAU) at its twenty-ninth ordinary session, held at Cairo in June

1993, the Committee urgently requested UNITA to comply with Security Council resolutions 851 (1993) and 864 (1994).

Burundi

14.   The Committee expressed its concern at the lack of security and the violence and mass killings in Burundi, which were exacerbated by politico-ethnic rivalry.

15.   The Committee appealed to all its brothers in Burundi to work for national reconciliation and to ensure that their democratic gains were not reversed.

16.   The Committee invited the member States to demonstrate their solidarity by encouraging the efforts made at the national, subregional, regional and international levels.

17.   The Committee commended its officers for the positions they had taken in October 1993 and March 1994, when they had condemned the violence responsible for the loss of human lives, including that of President Melchior Ndadaye, and had called on the United Nations and OAU to do everything possible to promote a return to constitutional order, an end to the sufferings of the civilian population and engagement in dialogue and consultation.

Rwanda

18.   The Committee invited its Rwandese brothers to implement the Arusha Peace Agreement of 4 August 1993 with a view to expediting national reconciliation and the establishment of the democratic institutions provided for in that Agreement.

Cameroon

19.   With regard to the territorial and border dispute between Cameroon and Nigeria, the Committee expressed grave concern at the tension in the Bakassi peninsula and its potential for degeneration into armed conflict.

20.   The Committee welcomed the steps taken by Cameroon to settle the dispute peacefully by, inter alia, referring the matter to the Central Organ of the OAU Mechanism for Conflict Prevention, Management and Resolution in Africa and to the Security Council and the International Court of Justice. It requested those bodies to deal urgently with the dispute.

21.   The Committee commended the Central Organ's reaffirmation of principles, at its meeting on 24 March 1994, with regard to inviolability of borders inherited from colonial times, respect for national sovereignty and independence, and peaceful settlement of disputes.

22.   The Committee took note of the appeal by the OAU Central Organ inviting the parties to exercise restraint and to take appropriate steps to rebuild confidence by, for example, considering the withdrawal of troops and continuing the dialogue.

23.   The Committee expressed its solidarity with Cameroon in the crisis and urged the parties to give precedence to dialogue and good faith in the search for a peaceful solution based on international law.

(a)   Problem of arms proliferation among members of the civilian population

24.   The Committee expressed its concern about the proliferation of arms among members of the civilian population and invited all the member States of the subregion to take the necessary measures, including collective action, to curb that destabilizing trend.

25.   The Committee instructed its officers to approach the United Nations Secretary-General to request assistance to that end.

(b) Specific recommendations

26. In the light of the foregoing situations and requests, the Committee recommended that its officers should carry out the following action and report to it at its fifth meeting:

(a) Inform the Secretary-General of OAU and the Government of Burundi that member States would be willing to participate in the observer missions requested by fraternal Burundi;

(b) Inform the Secretary-General of the United Nations and the Government of Rwanda that member States would be willing to participate in any of the international observer missions in Rwanda;

(c) Support all steps taken at the regional, multilateral and international levels to settle the Cameroon-Nigeria dispute peacefully.

27. The Committee instructed its officers to convey all the above recommendations to the United Nations Secretary-General, for transmittal to the Security Council and the General Assembly.

2. Reflections on ways and means to achieve the peaceful settlement of crises and conflicts in Central Africa

3. Preventive diplomacy in Central Africa: exchange of views

4. Towards a common defence in Central Africa: exchange of views

5. Elaboration of measures for promoting the establishment of a standing inter-State general staff for crisis management with a view to setting up a subregional peace-keeping force

28. After a lengthy discussion of the four mutually reinforcing and complementary issues, in which the States members of the Committee confirmed their willingness to move towards the goal of their common defence in stages, the Committee concluded that the deliberations were sufficiently advanced and that the time was ripe to take action by implementing the following recommendations:

(a) The current Chairman of the Committee should prevail upon the 11 heads of State and Government of the subregion to sign promptly the Non-Aggression Pact adopted at Libreville at the third meeting of the Committee and should report to the latter at its fifth meeting;

(b) The delegations of the Congo and Zaire should draw up two draft legal instruments, one relating to a protocol of mutual assistance among the member States of the subregion in the area of defence and the other to the special status of a model unit specializing in peace-keeping missions with a view to the establishment of such a unit within the armed forces of each member State. The two drafts should be submitted to the Committee at its fifth meeting;

(c) The delegations of Cameroon and Chad should carry out a study of the typology of crises and conflicts in the subregion in which the intervention of a collective security mechanism might be required. The study should also be submitted to the Committee at its fifth meeting;

(d) The delegation of Gabon should prepare a draft on the organization of a temporary general staff committee for crisis management in the subregion. The draft should be submitted to the Committee at its fifth meeting;

(e) Each State member of the Committee should set up a national body to follow up the Committee's activities. A report on the establishment of such a body should be submitted to the Committee at its fifth meeting.

6. Review of procedural questions and questions relating to the work of the current officers of the Committee

29. The discussion of procedural questions and questions relating to the work of the officers of the Committee focused on the streamlining of activities. The Committee agreed on the following measures:

(a) The Committee's agenda and programme of work should, in future, be submitted separately. The draft agenda should be transmitted to member States at least one month before the convening of the Committee;

(b) As the Committee was operating under the auspices of the United Nations General Assembly, its recommendations should take the form of declarations or resolutions;

(c) Given that the tasks to be entrusted to its officers would be more practical in future, the Committee recommended that the States which provided the officers should be responsible for the financial efforts required for the performance of those tasks;

(d) It was agreed in principle that the term of the officers of the Committee should be extended from 6 to 12 months but that the six-monthly periodicity of Committee meetings should be maintained. The country providing the Chairman should act as host to two consecutive meetings of the Committee;

(e) The Committee agreed to include in the agenda of its next meeting an item on the status of observers and those invited to attend its meetings.

7. Miscellaneous

30. With a view to strengthening security, stability and development in the countries of the subregion by further promoting respect for human rights and the establishment of democracy, the Committee was of the view that a subregional centre for human rights should be set up at Yaoundé under the auspices of the Centre for Human Rights of the United Nations Secretariat.

31. Such action would be pursuant to the implementation of the Declaration and Programme of Action adopted by the World Conference on Human Rights, which was held at Vienna from 14 to 25 June 1993.

32. The subregional centre for human rights would be concerned above all with helping to train staff engaged in administering human rights matters, extending support to the establishment or strengthening of national human rights institutions and assisting in the dissemination and popularization of international human rights instruments.

33. Further to the recommendation at its third meeting regarding the participation in the Committee's meetings of subregional economic integration organizations (the Economic Community of Central African States (ECCAS), the Central African Customs and Economic Union (CACEU) and the Economic Community of the Great Lakes (CEPGL)), and in view of those organizations' financial difficulties, the Committee decided that, whenever participation was not feasible, those organizations would in future be represented by the delegation of the State which provided the current Chairman.

34. The Committee welcomed the establishment by the Government of Chad of a national commission to study the typology of crises and conflicts in Central Africa.

35. The Committee was also pleased to note the decision of the Libyan Government to withdraw its troops from the Aouzou Strip, pursuant to the Judgment delivered by the International Court of Justice, on 3 February

1994.

8. Submission, consideration and adoption of the final report on the fourth meeting of the Committee

36. The final report on the fourth meeting of the Standing Advisory Committee on Security Questions in Central Africa was unanimously adopted on 8 April 1994 by the ministerial meeting.

37. The Committee decided to hold its fifth meeting at Yaoundé in the second half of 1994, at a time to be determined by its officers.

III. FIFTH MEETING OF THE STANDING ADVISORY COMMITTEE ON SECURITY QUESTIONS IN CENTRAL AFRICA

38. The fifth meeting of the Standing Advisory Committee on Security Questions in Central Africa was held at Yaoundé, from 5 to 7 September 1994 at the expert level and on 8 and 9 September 1994 at the ministerial level.

39. Ten delegations from the 11 States members of the Committee took part in the meeting: Angola, Burundi, Cameroon, Central African Republic, Chad, Congo, Equatorial Guinea, Gabon, Sao Tome and Principe and Zaire.

40. Rwanda was unable to send a delegation.

41. At the opening ceremony of the ministerial meeting, statements were made by Mr. Edouard Akame Mfoumou, Minister of Defence attached to the Office of the President, representing the host country; Mr. Sammy Kum Buo, Secretary of the Committee; and Mr. Ferdinand Léopold Oyono, Minister for Foreign Affairs of Cameroon, current Chairman of the Committee.

A. Progress of work

1. Reports by individual delegations on steps taken to establish a national body to follow up the Committee's activities

42. After the individual delegations had reported, the Committee concluded that progress had been made with respect to the establishment by each member State of a national body to follow up the Committee's activities. It commended the measures taken by some of the States and invited others to emulate the examples of Cameroon and the Congo.

2. Observer participation in the Committee's meetings

43. After considering the question, the Committee accepted the principle of observer participation in its meetings.

44. The Committee accorded permanent observer status to the subregional economic integration organizations (ECCAS, CACEU, CEPGL) and to OAU.

45. It decided that other States Members of the United Nations, States members of international organizations and non-governmental organizations, research establishments and any natural or legal person concerned with the promotion of international peace and security would be able to participate in its meetings upon their request and subject to the officers' agreement.

46. The Committee reiterated its intention to invite, when necessary, any natural or legal person to participate in its meetings as an expert or a consultant.

3. Review of the geopolitical and security situation in the Central African subregion

47. Following an exchange of views on this subject, the Committee noted that the situation in Central Africa had worsened

dramatically since its fourth meeting, with particularly tragic consequences in Rwanda.

48. Given the uncertainties, the Committee made the following recommendations.

Angola

49. As regards progress in Angola, the Committee expressed its concern at the duration of the current talks at Lusaka which had already lasted nine months because of the intransigence of UNITA.

50. It invited once more its Angolan brothers to take advantage of the talks to reach a prompt, just, equitable and durable solution conducive to the restoration of peace in their country.

51. The Committee renewed its support for the Government of Angola and expressed encouragement for that Government's efforts at the bilateral and multilateral levels to reach a negotiated solution, and it emphasized once again the importance of the Declaration on the situation in Angola adopted by the OAU Conference of Heads of State and Government at its twenty-ninth ordinary session and the declarations on Angola adopted by the Central Organ of the OAU Mechanism for Conflict Prevention, Management and Resolution in Africa.

52. The Committee commended the Republic of the Congo for its implementation of Security Council resolution 864 (1994) imposing a ban on the transit of arms and logistical support through the territory of Angola's neighbours. It invited the other neighbouring countries to follow suit.

Burundi

53. In the light of developments in Burundi, the Committee focused its attention on the Government's efforts to restore peace, promote national reconciliation and secure its borders.

54. The Committee called upon the international community to support national reconciliation and reconstruction efforts in Burundi.

55. It expressed interest in and support for the Burundi delegation's suggestion that the United Nations might be asked to organize an international conference on peace, security and development in the area of the Great Lakes Countries. It urged the Government of Burundi to follow up that suggestion.

Rwanda

56. With regard to Rwanda, which was in the throes of an unprecedented human disaster, the Committee urged the international community to redouble efforts to help that country effect its national reconciliation and reconstruction in as short a period as possible, so as to enable it to return to a state of normality.

57. The Committee commended the assistance provided by neighbouring countries to the fraternal Rwandese people, especially by Zaire.

58. It also commended those of its members which had sent military contingents to deliver humanitarian assistance to Rwanda (Chad and Congo) or had provided material and financial support (Gabon).

59. The Committee invited the other States of the subregion to continue to express their solidarity with the Rwandese people in a practical form.

60. The Committee urged Rwanda and Zaire to continue the recently begun bilateral talks with a view to promoting the return of refugees to their homes. It took note of the Zairian delegation's expression of concern and its request for support from the international community in order to cope with the problems caused by the arrival of

waves of Rwandese refugees in its territory, a situation which posed a real threat to the security of Zaire and of other neighbouring countries.

Other member States

Cameroon

61. As to the territorial and border dispute between Cameroon and Nigeria, the Committee, while reiterating its solidarity with Cameroon, welcomed the resumption of summit-level talks between the two States, with Togo as mediator and with support from the international community, and urged them to continue such efforts.

Other States

62. The Committee commended the current peace efforts in Chad, the Congo, Gabon and Zaire and called for their strengthening.

63. In view of the climate of uncertainty and danger in the subregion, the Committee recommended that its officers should visit Angola, Burundi and Rwanda on a mission of solidarity before the end of the current term.

Specific recommendations addressed to the officers of the Committee

64. Given the financial efforts required of the States members providing the officers of the Committee, the Committee recommended that when a member State acted as host to a delegation of officers of the Committee, it should provide that delegation with accommodation and transport within its borders.

65. Such contribution by the host country related especially to the Chairman and/or another officer of the Committee.

66. The Committee agreed to include in the agenda of every meeting an item entitled "Evaluation of the recommendations made at the preceding meeting".

4. Group discussion on the theme "Crises and conflicts in Central Africa: the role to be played by and the outlook for preventive diplomacy"

67. A group discussion on the theme "Crises and conflicts in Central Africa: the role to be played by and the outlook for preventive diplomacy" marked the closure of the expert proceedings. In addition to the delegations participating in the meeting, invitations to attend were issued to members of the host Government and the diplomatic corps, representatives of international organizations, and other eminent persons. The group heard a statement by Mr. Shawn McCormick, Deputy Director, Africa Division, Center for Strategic Studies, Washington, on the role and contribution of foreign actors in the peaceful conflict resolution in Central Africa and a statement by Mr. Assane Fall Diop, Journalist, Radio France internationale, Paris, on the role of the media in armed conflict resolution in Africa. In the ensuing debate, many points of substance were raised as participants exchanged views on current crises and conflicts in the subregion, including the question of measures aimed at their prevention. It was decided that the exercise had provided food for thought in the Committee's pursuit of a better understanding of the crises and conflicts afflicting the subregion.

5. Submission of draft studies

68. The following four draft studies were before the Committee:

(a) Typology of sources of crises and conflicts in Central Africa (submitted by the delegations of Cameroon and Chad);

(b) Mutual assistance agreement with respect to defence and security between the States members of ECCAS (submitted by the delegations of the Congo and Zaire);

(c) Special status of the model unit specializing in peace-keeping missions (submitted by the delegations of the Congo and Zaire);

(d) Temporary general staff for crisis management in Central Africa (submitted by the delegation of Gabon).

69. After a fruitful exchange of views on the four draft studies, the Committee expressed its satisfaction with the high quality of the work accomplished and the relevance of the studies, and decided to continue consideration of them at its sixth meeting. It paid homage to its experts.

70. The States members of the Committee renewed their commitment to participation in peace-keeping operations within the framework of the United Nations and OAU.

71. To that end, they undertook to establish within their respective armed forces a unit specializing in peace-keeping operations.

72. They asked for assistance from the United Nations, OAU and third States in the training and preparation of such units and in establishing an appropriate system for managing security problems in Central Africa.

73. The Committee recommended that its Secretary and officers should become more deeply involved in the search for ways to enable the Committee to achieve its goals.

6. Initialling of the Non-Aggression Pact between the States members of the Economic Community of Central African States

74. At the Committee's fifth meeting, the member States initialled the Non-Aggression Pact concluded by the States members of the Economic Community of Central African States. All

the delegations said that they regarded the Pact as a milestone in the context of the continuing efforts by the countries members of the Committee in the area of preventive diplomacy. At the ministerial meeting, the Chairman of the Committee announced that the heads of State of the subregion could be expected to sign the Pact before the end of the current year and emphasized the need for its entry into force without delay.

7. Submission, consideration and adoption of the final report on the fifth meeting of the Committee

75. The final report on the fifth meeting of the Standing Advisory Committee on Security Questions in Central Africa was adopted unanimously by the ministerial meeting.

76. The sixth meeting of the Standing Advisory Committee on Security Questions in Central Africa will be held at Brazzaville during the first half of 1995, at a time yet to be determined.

IV. CONCLUSION

77. Central Africa continues to experience strife and open conflict, particularly in Angola, Burundi and Rwanda. It is therefore incumbent on the Secretary-General to congratulate the member countries which have already provided assistance, of one kind or another, to those three countries. The tragic events in Angola and Burundi and, more especially, in Rwanda have once again underlined as a necessity, as the Committee has pointed out, that all possible ways of curbing crises before they degenerate into open conflicts should be explored in a sustained manner.

78. The Non-Aggression Pact adopted unanimously by the States members of the Committee in 1993, and recently initialled, is undoubtedly a practical result of considerable impact. The prompt signature and entry into force of the Pact will certainly

help to attenuate many of the differences between States. It is therefore a positive beginning, but much remains to be done both to consolidate the progress made through agreement on the Pact and to develop and implement internal measures conducive to the promotion of veritable peace and security in each of the States of the subregion.

79. The decision of the countries members of the Committee to establish, within their respective armed forces, units specializing in peace-keeping, is a positive development which will promote their effective participation in peace-keeping operations. Appropriate measures to strengthen the implementation of this decision should be taken as soon as possible.

80. The Secretary-General is convinced that the extremely useful work already initiated within the framework of the Committee again deserves the continuing support and encouragement of the international community.

A/50/474

I. INTRODUCTION

1. By its resolution 49/76 C of 15 December 1994, the General Assembly, inter alia, requested me to submit to it at its fiftieth session a report on the work of the Standing Advisory Committee on Security Questions in Central Africa. The present report, focusing on the sixth and seventh ministerial meetings of the Committee, is in fulfilment of that request.

2. Both meetings were held at Brazzaville, the first from 20 to 24 March and the second from 28 August to 1 September 1995. Mr. Wilfrid de Souza, Director of the Africa II Division of the Department of Political Affairs, and Mr. Alioune Blondin Beye, my Special Representative in Angola,

represented me and at the sixth and seventh meetings, respectively and delivered a message on my behalf. A message from the Secretary-General of the Organization of African Unity was delivered at each of the meetings by his representative. Both meetings were chaired by His Excellency General Joachim Yhombi Opango, Prime Minister and head of Government of the Congo.

3. At the sixth meeting the following officers were elected to conduct the work of the Committee for a period of one year: Congo, President; Angola, First Vice-President; Zaire, Second Vice-President; Equatorial Guinea, Rapporteur.

II. PROCEEDINGS OF THE SIXTH AND SEVENTH MEETINGS

4. During the sixth and the seventh ministerial meetings, the Committee focused its work on the following main areas: (a) review of the Central African geopolitical and security situation; (b) consideration of the study on the typology of the sources of crises and conflicts in Central Africa; (c) consideration of the draft protocol on mutual assistance on defence and security matters and of the draft statute of a model unit for peace-keeping operations in Central Africa; (d) consideration of the establishment of a non-permanent general staff for crisis management in Central Africa; and (e) consideration of a draft budget for the Committee.

A. Review of the geopolitical and security situation in Central Africa

5. It has become an established practice for the Committee to review the geopolitical and security situation in the subregion at each of its meetings with a view to seeking practical ways and means of addressing existing or potentially conflictual problems in each of the countries concerned.

6. After an exchange of views on the subject, the Committee noted that the security situation in Central Africa had improved somewhat since last year. It observed, however, that Burundi and Rwanda continued to be sources of much concern. The delegation of Rwanda expressed reservations with regard to that assessment of the situation in the country.

7. The Committee welcomed the adoption on 28 August 1995 of Security Council resolution 1012 (1995), on the creation of an international commission of inquiry to establish the facts relating to the assassination of the President of Burundi on 21 October 1993, the massacres and other related serious acts of violence which followed. Furthermore, the Committee noted with satisfaction the initiative taken by the Organization of African Unity to promote the restoration of peace and security in the subregion, particularly in Burundi, by means of diplomatic measures and a military mission.

8. The Committee welcomed the steps taken by the authorities in Cameroon, the Central African Republic and Chad to halt the activities of highway bandits. It also welcomed the significant progress made in Angola in implementing the Lusaka Protocols. It welcomed the return to a state of constitutionality in Sao Tome and Principe, following the attempted coup d'état that had taken place in that country.

9. The Committee began an exchange of views on the topic of foreign intervention for humanitarian purposes in the subregion on the basis of a paper submitted by the delegation of Congo. It decided to defer further consideration of the item to the eighth meeting.

10. The question of the proliferation of light weapons in the subregion has been under constant consideration in the Committee. The spread of such weapons, including among the civilian population and other

armed groups in the countries of the subregion, has contributed to the existence and exacerbation of conflicts in the area and undermined the efforts of Governments to ensure security, law and order and sustainable development. In the context of the sixth ministerial meeting, a presentation was made on this subject by Mr. William Eteki-Mboumoua, former Secretary-General of the Organization of African Unity, in his capacity as head of my Advisory Mission on the Proliferation of Light Weapons in the Sahara-Sahel subregion. The Committee has decided, in this connection, to convene at a future date a meeting of the Ministers of Defence and the Interior of member States to examine the issues involved in greater depth.

11. Discussions have been held on the subject of a subregional arms register and on the need for promoting transparency. The need for effective control of the illicit flow of arms has also been expressed in this context. Many believed that the establishment of an arms register within the Committee that would take into account data such as force levels and light weapons would be a valid contribution to the existing United Nations Register of Conventional Arms. In the view of many delegations, the Register in its present form is too restrictive in the categories of weapons with which it is concerned.

12. At its seventh meeting, the Committee adopted the Brazzaville Declaration on Cooperation for Peace and Security in Central Africa. In the Declaration, member States express their deep concern at the persistence of tensions and violence in the subregion and outline a number of measures aimed at improving the situation. These measures include the holding of one of the Committee's forthcoming meetings at United Nations Headquarters in order to allow for a broader exchange of views with United Nations organs and bodies involved in the search for solutions to the problems of the subregion. The text of the Declaration is

attached as Annex I to the present report.

B. Review of the draft study on the typology of sources of crises and conflict

13. The typology, based on a study carried out by Cameroon and Chad at the request of the Committee, was adopted at the sixth meeting. The study, which is attached as annex II to the present report, draws on the recent experiences of the countries of Central Africa with regard to sources of tensions, crises and conflicts at the domestic, inter-State and international levels.

C. Draft protocol on mutual assistance on defence and security matters and the statute of a model unit specializing in peace-keeping missions

14. At the seventh meeting the delegations of Congo and Zaire submitted the study they had been requested to carry out at the fourth meeting in 1994. The Committee took note of the draft text submitted by the two countries and deferred consideration on it to the eighth meeting in order to allow member States the opportunity to study it in depth.

15. With regard to the statute of a model unit specializing in peace-keeping operations, to be established within the armed forces of member States, the Committee adopted the terms of reference proposed by Congo and Zaire at the sixth meeting. It strongly encouraged other member States to proceed with the establishment of such units, following the examples of Equatorial Guinea, Chad and Zaire. Such units, it was pointed out, could be made available for peace-keeping operations when needed, especially in the subregion. The Secretary-General was requested to provide United Nations assistance in training personnel for the units.

D. Consideration of the establishment of a non-permanent general staff for crisis management

16. At its seventh meeting the Committee completed its consideration of the item, taking into account in particular the study carried out on the topic by the delegation of Gabon. It adopted the proposal and assigned the task of gathering information and data on crises to the national committees set up in each member State to follow up the work of the Committee. The Bureau of the Committee was charged with the responsibility of coordinating the work of the national committees in this field.

E. Consideration of the budget of the Bureau

17. The Committee commended the efforts made by the delegation of Congo to prepare a draft budget for the Bureau of the Committee, following a recommendation made at the sixth meeting. The consideration and adoption of the budget estimate was postponed to the eighth meeting. In the meantime, a trust fund in the amount of 11 million CFA francs, or 1 million from each State, was opened so that the President of the Bureau could, as called for by the Committee, undertake the missions of solidarity in the countries in conflict in the subregion. It was decided that the fund should be endowed by 31 March 1996 and should be open to voluntary contributions from member States and any other interested donors within or outside the region.

III. CONCLUSIONS AND OBSERVATIONS

18. Deep-seated problems continue to afflict Central Africa, threatening its stability and its future. The two meetings of the Committee in 1995 again offered a valuable opportunity for States members of the Committee to take decisions which, if combined with the requisite political will and practical measures, should strengthen the

chances of peace and reduce those of war in the subregion.

19. It is vital, therefore, for the Governments concerned to translate into concrete actions their stated commitments to peace and cooperation and the various recommendations and decisions they have adopted to that end. The Brazzaville Declaration on Cooperation for Peace and Security in Central Africa, adopted at the Committee's seventh meeting, represents another important step forward in the Committee's quest for a better and brighter future for Central Africa. But its real value and significance will be determined by the extent to which the measures it contains are implemented.

20. The high cost of conflicts in the subregion, both financially and in human terms, underlines the need for bolder steps to prevent future turmoil. This will require patience, moderation and tolerance on the part of all, both at the domestic and at the inter-State levels. The role of the United Nations has been to provide a mechanism through which the countries of the area can seek to harmonize their strategies for peace and mutual confidence. The primary responsibility for using that mechanism to good effect rests with the countries themselves.

21. I welcome the responsibility and seriousness shown by the Central African countries in their attempt to deal with the increasingly complex and multidimensional nature of the challenges facing the subregion including, in particular, the refugee and other humanitarian aspects. Many of these countries, in particular Zaire, have welcomed on their territories large numbers of refugees uprooted by conflict in neighbouring States. The growing problem of refugees and displaced persons in the subregion is not only a human tragedy but also a potential danger to security and sustainable development. It must be addressed in its totality. I encourage

Member States to support the efforts of my Special Envoy for the Great Lakes Region of Central Africa, Ambassador José Luis Jesús, who is carrying out consultations on preparations for the convening of a conference on security, stability and development in the area.

22. I remain convinced that the Committee is an instrument that can contribute substantially to the restoration of peace and security in this part of Africa. I remain concerned, however, about the risk that continued non-implementation of decisions and measures agreed upon by the Committee will impair its effectiveness.

ANNEX I

(For the text of the Brazzaville Declaration on Cooperation for Peace and Security in Central Africa, see "Other Documents", page 81.)

ANNEX II

(For the text of the Typology of Sources of Conflict in the Central African Subregion, see "Other Documents", page 97.)

A/51/287

I. INTRODUCTION

1. By its resolution 50/71 B of 12 December 1995, the General Assembly, inter alia, reaffirmed its support for the programme of work of the Standing Advisory Committee on Security Questions in Central Africa and urged States members of the Committee to implement the specific measures they had already adopted within the framework of the Committee's work programme. The Assembly also requested me to continue to provide assistance to States members of the Committee and to report to the Assembly at its fifty-first session on the implementation of the resolution. The

present report, focusing on the activities of the Committee in the period since the adoption of resolution 50/71 B, is submitted in fulfilment of that request.

2. During the reporting period, the work of the Committee intensified and expanded significantly. Consultations and more formal meetings took place at various levels as States members of the Committee continued to address the persistent threats to peace and security in the Central African subregion with a view to promoting sustainable measures of confidence-building and arms restraint and preventing further turmoil in the area.

3. I followed developments in the subregion closely and attended in person the first meeting of heads of State and Government of States members of the Committee which was held at Yaoundé on 8 July 1996. I reaffirmed to the Committee the support of the United Nations for its goals and objectives. On 23 June 1996, prior to the summit, I met at Geneva with Mr. Destin Arsène Tsaty-Boungou, Foreign Minister of the Congo, in his capacity as President of the Bureau of the Committee. He briefed me on the Committee's priorities and plans with regard to the implementation of its programme of work. In addition, Mr. Prvoslav Davinić, Director of the Centre for Disarmament Affairs in the Department of Political Affairs of the Secretariat, represented me at the Committee's eighth ministerial meeting held at Yaoundé from 15 to 19 April 1996, and delivered a statement on my behalf. That meeting was chaired by His Excellency Mr. Simon Achidi Achu, Prime Minister and Head of Government of Cameroon. The Secretariat also provided substantive support to the ministerial meeting of the Committee's Bureau held at Brazzaville on 14 and 15 June 1996.

II. PROCEEDINGS OF THE MINISTERIAL AND SUMMIT MEETINGS OF THE COMMITTEE IN 1996

4. Concern over continued tensions and conflict in the subregion and the seemingly growing threat that the situations of violence and instability could deteriorate further, especially in the Great Lakes area, greatly influenced the discussions of the Committee during the reporting period. It was recognized from the outset of the eighth ministerial meeting that the increasingly dangerous situation in the subregion needed to be examined by member States at the highest political level with a view to evolving a concrete subregional plan of action.

5. Both at the eighth ministerial meeting at Yaoundé and at the Bureau meeting at Brazzaville, it was felt that while the primary responsibility for resolving the political and security problems in the Central African subregion rested with the Governments and peoples of the countries concerned, concerted action at the subregional and wider levels was required to promote lasting solutions. The summit meeting therefore offered a historic opportunity to begin to chart a strategy for effective subregional cooperation on issues of peace and security. At the same time, the ministers reaffirmed the important need for continued and intensified international support, especially for efforts to halt the proliferation of weapons in Central Africa, to diffuse potentially catastrophic situations and to meet the critical humanitarian needs of millions of refugees and displaced persons in the area.

6. At their meeting on 8 July 1996, the heads of State and Government of Committee member States set out a course of action on subregional security cooperation and outlined a number of specific measures to be taken to that end. They emphasized the urgent need to avert future conflicts, both within and between

States in the subregion.

7. Among the specific measures agreed upon by the heads of State and Government were the following:

(a) The creation, promotion and support of good governance and participatory democracy;

(b) The organization, under United Nations auspices, of seminars to promote a sustainable culture of peace and democratic responsibility within the armed forces, the paramilitary forces (gendarmerie) and the police forces of States members of the Standing Advisory Committee;

(c) The adoption and implementation of subregional confidence-building measures, including in particular the signature and effective observance of the Non-Aggression Pact among Central African States;

(d) The implementation, with the assistance of the United Nations and the international community as a whole, of a disarmament programme designed to deal with the problem of the uncontrolled proliferation of weapons;

(e) The establishment, under United Nations auspices, of a subregional early-warning mechanism to monitor developments in Central Africa with a view to preventing potential crises or tensions from degenerating into armed conflicts;

(f) The designation, within the armed forces and the paramilitary and police forces of States members of the Committee, of specialized units for possible deployment with United Nations and/or Organization of African Unity (OAU) peace missions;

(g) The convening, on a regular basis, of meetings of heads of State and Government, within the framework of the Standing Advisory Committee on Security

Questions in Central Africa, to examine peace and related security issues in the subregion.

8. At the summit, the heads of State and Government of the following eight States members of the Committee formally signed the Non-Aggression Pact: Burundi, Cameroon, Chad, Congo, Equatorial Guinea, Gabon, Sao Tome and Principe and Zaire. They also requested their ministers to elaborate, urgently and jointly, the practical modalities for an effective programme to curb the proliferation of weapons in Central Africa and to examine with United Nations officials concrete ways and means to bring the proposed early-warning mechanism into existence and to ensure its functioning.

9. Cognizant of the financial and other material resources required to implement fully and effectively their programme for subregional stability, the Central African leaders called for enhanced cooperation with bilateral and multilateral donors in a shared partnership for peace and security in the subregion. They conveyed their deep gratitude to those donors that had already contributed or planned to contribute to the trust fund set up by the United Nations to receive voluntary contributions to help finance the implementation of the programme of work of the Committee.

III. OTHER RELATED ACTIVITIES AND PROGRAMMES IN 1996

10. Member States continued to set up national committees to ensure effective follow-up at the national level to advance the work and the objectives of the Committee. They also continued to take the necessary practical steps to designate within their respective armed forces specialized units for possible deployment with future United Nations and/or OAU peace operations.

11. With regard to the peace units, the

General Assembly, by its resolution 50/71 B, welcomed with satisfaction the decision by the States members of the Committee to establish such units. It also welcomed the participation by some of those States in the peace operations deployed in the subregion and called upon States Members of the United Nations and governmental and non-governmental organizations to promote and to facilitate the holding of a training programme on peace operations in the subregion with a view to strengthening the capacity of such units. The Secretariat, in cooperation with the International Peace Academy and with funding from the Government of Japan, will shortly organize in Yaoundé, the first training programme on peace operations for senior military and civilian officials of Central African States. The session is designed to train officials who, upon their return home, would serve as instructors and help prepare the units set up within their respective national forces.

12. There were growing indications, in 1996, of increasing efforts to foster transparency and inter-State cooperation on military and security matters in the subregion. States members of the Committee, at their eighth ministerial meeting in April, agreed in principle on the confidence-building value of a subregional arms register to monitor weapons acquisitions and transfers in Central Africa with a view to their control and reduction. Stressing their conviction that instability in any African country threatened the security of the region as a whole, they also showed growing interest in contributing to the peaceful resolution of existing conflicts in Central Africa. Members of the Committee's Bureau plan to visit Angola, Burundi, Rwanda and Zaire to convey the support and encouragement of other Central African States to such efforts in Angola and the Great Lakes region. The President of the Bureau is also scheduled to hold discussions with the former Tanzanian President, Mwalimu Julius K. Nyerere, in his capacity as the OAU peace facilitator for the

Great Lakes region. The Committee has stressed the importance of a coordinated African response to facilitate the quest for a satisfactory solution to the complex problems in that part of the Central African subregion.

13. States members of the Standing Advisory Committee continued to reaffirm in 1996 their support for the democratization process in the subregion. In my meeting at Geneva on 23 June with the President of the Bureau, he informed me that members of the Committee, based on their conviction that lasting peace in the subregion would be facilitated in the long term under conditions of democracy and good governance, had decided to hold a subregional conference in December 1996 on the topic "Democratic institutions and peace in Central Africa". The meeting, scheduled to take place in Brazzaville, will examine, among other aspects, the rule of law and the role of the armed forces in a democratic system. The President of the Bureau also requested United Nations support and cooperation for the organization of the conference.

IV. ADMINISTRATIVE AND FINANCIAL ASPECTS

14. In its request to me to continue to provide assistance to States members of the Standing Advisory Committee, the General Assembly, in its resolution 50/71 B, also asked me to establish a trust fund to which States Members of the United Nations and governmental and non-governmental organizations might make additional voluntary contributions for the implementation of the programme of work of the Committee. On 18 March 1996, I established the United Nations Trust Fund for the Standing Advisory Committee on Security Questions in Central Africa and invited Member States and governmental and non-governmental organizations to contribute to it. States members of the Committee pledged, shortly thereafter, to contribute to the Trust Fund, which has

already received contributions from a number of Governments. The Governments of Cameroon and the Congo also made contributions in the form of material and other practical support for the organization of the Yaoundé summit on Central African security in July and the June meeting at Brazzaville of members of the Bureau of the Committee. In addition, the Government of Japan has made a contribution of $600,000 and several other Governments and organizations have indicated that they are considering the appeal for contributions.

15. In the face of the continuing financial crisis confronting the United Nations, ministerial meetings of the Committee have been reduced to one per year for the current biennium. Financial requirements for any additional meetings and activities during the biennium will have to be met from voluntary contributions.

V. CONCLUSIONS AND OBSERVATIONS

16. The first meeting at the level of heads of State and Government of the Standing Advisory Committee on Security Questions in Central Africa, and the Declaration issued on that occasion (A/51/274, annex), represent a milestone in the life of the Committee and in the quest for lasting peace and security in this turbulent subregion.

17. As developments in Burundi and throughout the Great Lakes region demonstrate, Central Africa continues, in 1996, to be confronted by enormous politico-military and security challenges undermining prospects for its socio-economic recovery and progress and threatening its long-term peace and stability. The political will shown by the subregional security summit was an unmistakable sign of commitment by States in the area to tackle at the highest political level and in a concerted manner the complex problems involved. I share the leaders' sense of concern and, indeed, anxiety. The

potentially explosive nature of conflicts in Central Africa means that instability in any part of the subregion could affect the security of the area as a whole.

18. By their signature of the Non-Aggression Pact, the reaffirmation of their commitment to disarmament and their decision to pursue the creation of a subregional early-warning mechanism, the heads of State and Government have laid a strong foundation for a more promising future for Central Africa. The signature of the Pact by all States in the subregion and the effective and concrete implementation of the decisions taken by the heads of State and Government would contribute to making the promise a reality. At the same time, I welcome the Standing Advisory Committee's collective recognition that the peace and security of the subregion can be assured in the long term only through respect for human rights, democratization, the rule of law and socio-economic development.

19. I greatly welcome and encourage the organization of the first training seminar in Central Africa to help prepare units designated by States members of the Committee for possible deployment in peace operations. I share the General Assembly's support for the decision by the States concerned to set up the units and to participate in future operations. That decision demonstrates a strong commitment by Central African countries to take concrete actions to promote subregional confidence-building and security cooperation. I also support the appeal to States Members of the United Nations and governmental and non-governmental organizations to help, through training, in strengthening the capacity of the Central African peace units and thus render them operational on short notice, when needed. I wish to express my deep appreciation and gratitude to the Government of Japan for its generous financial contribution which made the organization of the first training programme

possible and to the Government of Cameroon for hosting it and providing local logistical support.

20. The activities of the Standing Advisory Committee in 1996 have demonstrated, once again, that it is an instrument of much promise in efforts to end the scourge of violence and destruction in one of Africa's most unstable subregions. The Committee continues to show a great sense of responsibility and seriousness in handling delicate issues and challenges. It should therefore continue to receive the support and encouragement of the international community. I urge member States and the international community as a whole to contribute as generously as possible to the United Nations Trust Fund set up to enable the Committee implement its programme of work.

A/52/293

I. INTRODUCTION

1. By its resolution 51/46 C of 10 December 1996, the General Assembly reaffirmed its support for efforts aimed at promoting confidence-building measures at regional and subregional levels in order to ease tensions and conflicts in Central Africa and to further arms restraint and the peaceful settlement of disputes in that subregion. To that end, the Assembly, affirming its support for the programme of work of the Standing Advisory Committee on Security Questions in Central Africa, requested the Secretary-General to continue to provide assistance to the States members of the Committee and to report to it at its fifty-second session on the implementation of the resolution. The present report focuses on the activities of the Standing Advisory Committee since the submission, on 14 August 1996, of the Secretary-General's previous report to the Assembly at its fifty-first session (A/51/287).

2. As the people of Central Africa continued to pay a terrible price for political instability and conflict during the reporting period, I was encouraged by a growing readiness and determination by Central African States themselves to intensify their efforts with a view to preventing further turmoil in their subregion and promoting sustainable peace.

3. Recognizing that lasting peace in their area could not be imposed from outside, Central African countries increasingly consulted with each other and participated in several efforts at various levels to address the threats to peace and security in the subregion.

4. The United Nations has followed and supported those efforts. On 2 and 3 December 1996, Heads of State and Government of States members of the Standing Advisory Committee held an extraordinary summit meeting at Brazzaville to examine the persistent crises in the Great Lakes region of Central Africa, and especially in Zaire [2] (see S/1996/1006, annex). Mr. Alioune Blondin Beye, Special Representative of the Secretary-General in Angola, represented my predecessor at that meeting.

5. During my first official mission to Africa shortly after taking office as Secretary-General, I attended the summit meeting of the Central Organ of the Organization of African Unity (OAU) Mechanism for Conflict Prevention, Management and Resolution, which took place at Lomé on 26 March 1997 to tackle the crisis in Zaire. I called for peaceful negotiations and dialogue and stressed the need for a firm commitment to lasting peace and reconstruction based on democracy, the rule of law and respect for

---

[2] By a communication dated 20 May 1997, the Secretariat was informed by the Member State known formerly as "Zaire" that the name of the State had been changed on 17 May to "the Democratic Republic of the Congo".

human rights. I also sent my Special Representative for the Great Lakes, Mr. Mohamed Sahnoun, to Libreville to represent me at a regional summit organized there on 8 May 1997 by President El Hadj Omar Bongo, to pursue a peaceful political solution to the Zairian crisis.

6. Meanwhile, I met in New York on 12 February 1997 with Mr. Destin-Arsène Tsaty-Boungou, Foreign Minister of the Congo, who, in his capacity as President of the Bureau of the Standing Advisory Committee, briefed me on the Committee's work programme, including in particular plans to convene a subregional conference on the theme "Democratic institutions and peace in Central Africa". I supported the initiative, seeing it as a useful opportunity to promote respect for the rule of law in Central African countries and thus contribute to stability in the subregion. That conference, initially scheduled to take place at Brazzaville from 20 to 25 April 1997, was eventually postponed to a future date to be set by the Committee's Bureau, owing to the critical situation at that time in neighbouring Zaire.

7. Furthermore, in response to an invitation from the Government of Gabon, I asked Mr. Sahnoun to represent me at the Committee's ninth ministerial meeting, which was held at Libreville from 7 to 11 July 1997, and to deliver a statement on my behalf. At that meeting, which was chaired by Mr. Paulin Obame Nguema, Prime Minister and Head of Government of Gabon, the Standing Advisory Committee elected new members for its Bureau as follows: President, Gabon; First Vice-President, Angola; Second Vice-President, Chad; and Rapporteur, Burundi. The Secretariat continued to provide substantive and organizational support for the various activities of the Committee, including the December 1996 Brazzaville summit and the July 1997 Libreville ministerial meeting.

II. PROCEEDINGS OF THE COMMITTEE'S MINISTERIAL MEETING IN 1997

8. Concern over persistent tensions and hostilities in the subregion, and especially over the ongoing conflict in the Congo and the peace process in the Central African Republic, dominated the Committee's ninth ministerial meeting. Ten of the Committee's 11 member States participated in the meeting; Rwanda was absent.

9. While deploring the fact that violence had continued to spread in the area as demonstrated by the outbreak, in June 1997, of armed hostilities in Brazzaville, participants nevertheless welcomed what they saw as positive and encouraging improvements in a number of other Central African States. In that connection, they specifically welcomed the fact that calm had returned to the Democratic Republic of the Congo and that the embargo on Burundi had been partially lifted. The meeting also called for the total elimination of sanctions on Burundi and for United Nations peace operations to be set up in the Congo and in the Central African Republic to help resolve the conflict situations there.

10. In addition to examining effective ways and means to resolve existing crises, delegates discussed in detail how to prevent conflicts from starting in the first place. They stressed the view that prevention was more effective, more attainable and significantly less costly than attempting to manage or resolve crises once they had degenerated into armed confrontations. They therefore called for concrete action to establish and to ensure the effective functioning, at the earliest possible date, of the early warning mechanism for Central Africa which the Heads of State and Government, at their July and December 1996 summit meetings at Yaoundé and Brazzaville, respectively, had decided to set up under the auspices of the Standing Advisory Committee.

11. The ministerial meeting also called for effective action against illicit arms transfers and circulation in Central Africa as a way of helping to prevent outbreaks of armed conflicts in the subregion. Delegates stressed, in that connection, that in addition to controlling weapons, attention should be paid to reducing the armed forces. In that regard, they urged international support for programmes initiated by Central African States themselves to retrain demobilized fighters in order to help ensure their smooth reintegration into civilian life.

12. Once again, participants recognized the usefulness of effective confidence-building measures among Central African States in the field of security as a means of enhancing inter-State cooperation deemed vital for meaningful progress for sustainable peace and stability in the subregion. They appealed to all States members of the Committee to sign the Non-Aggression Pact and to respect fully its provisions. They also agreed that regular meetings between their senior military and security officials, as well as joint military exercises and patrols and participation in subregional or regional peace operations, would help not only to tackle specific concerns such as controlling the illicit trade in arms and drugs and helping to resolve specific conflicts, but also to enhance overall transparency and confidence among Central African States.

13. Participants reiterated the view that while the primary responsibility for resolving the subregion's political and security problems rested with their respective countries, support from the international community as a whole would help to ensure lasting success for various peace efforts. Against that background, participants exchanged views with the representatives of four permanent members of the Security Council on ways and means of strengthening cooperation between the Council and Central African States in the maintenance of peace and security in the subregion. The permanent members had

been invited to the ninth ministerial meeting by the host Government.

14. At the meeting, the representatives of four of the permanent members of the Security Council (the United Kingdom of Great Britain and Northern Ireland did not send a representative) stressed, in particular, the importance of preventive efforts to avert future armed conflicts in the subregion and outlined measures and programmes their countries had initiated to support peace efforts in Central Africa. In that connection, France and the United States of America informed participants of a programme launched jointly with the United Kingdom to strengthen the capacity of African States to participate more effectively in peace operations in the region.

15. States members of the Committee appealed to the international community to support the Committee's various efforts to enhance stability in the subregion, including, in particular, their initiative to establish at Libreville a subregional early warning mechanism aimed at preventing future armed conflicts in Central Africa.

III. PROGRAMMES AND ACTIVITIES FOR 1997/98 REQUIRING VOLUNTARY CONTRIBUTIONS

16. The Committee, at its ninth ministerial meeting, agreed to carry out a number of programmes and activities for the remainder of 1997 and into early 1998. (See A/52/283-S/1997/644, annex, for the full report of the ninth ministerial meeting of the United Nations Standing Advisory Committee on Security Questions in Central Africa). Those activities would be funded from voluntary contributions. It is to be recalled that at the request of the General Assembly the Secretary-General, in March 1996, established a trust fund within the Secretariat to receive contributions which Member States and intergovernmental and non-governmental organizations might wish to make in support of the programme of

work of the Standing Advisory Committee. The specific programmes and activities adopted by the Committee for 1997/98 include the following:

(a) Establishment and functioning of an early warning mechanism for Central Africa (Committee members have decided to set up the mechanism at the earliest opportunity, if possible before the end of 1997, at Libreville);

(b) Launching of programmes for the retraining and reintegration of demobilized troops into civilian life;

(c) Controlling the illicit trade in arms and drugs in the subregion;

(d) Organization of training seminars to enhance the capacity of Central African States to participate in peace operations (the first such seminar for Central African States, organized with funding from the Government of Japan, was held at Yaoundé in September 1996);

(e) Organization of joint military exercises for peace operations;

(f) Organizing seminars and sensitization programmes on good governance, the rule of law and respect for human rights for military and security personnel of Central African States;

(g) Convening a subregional conference on the theme "Democratic institutions and peace in Central Africa" (the Government of Equatorial Guinea has offered to host the conference, which, depending upon the availability of voluntary contributions, is scheduled to take place in December 1997).

IV. ADMINISTRATIVE AND FINANCIAL ASPECTS

17. Member States will recall that from the outset, the Committee held two annual ministerial meetings, funded from the regular budget, to implement activities contained in its programme of work. However, owing to the financial crisis, the Committee held only one annual meeting each during 1996 and 1997. At the Committee's ninth ministerial meeting, member States called for the reinstatement of the two annual ministerial meetings to meet the growing need for discussions and other efforts to address the persistent crises in the subregion.

18. I wish to take this opportunity to express the gratitude and appreciation of the United Nations to those States that have contributed to the Trust Fund of the Committee and to appeal once again to all States as well as to intergovernmental and non-governmental organizations to continue and indeed to increase their support for the Committee's valuable efforts to promote confidence and stability in the volatile Central African subregion. I would also like to thank the Government of Gabon for the important contribution it made in facilitating the smooth convening at Libreville of the ninth ministerial meeting.

V. CONCLUSIONS AND OBSERVATIONS

19. Central Africa remains an area of much turbulence and suffering. But it is also one of the continent's most richly endowed subregions, with a vibrant population that yearns for a better life. Yet that goal can be realized only in a climate of lasting peace, which in turn depends on the will of the States and the people of the subregion.

20. In the period under review, the international community welcomed the return of stability to the Democratic Republic of the Congo, which has enormous implications for broader subregional peace and progress. But that was offset by the eruption of political violence in the neighbouring Republic of the Congo, where the situation remains unstable despite untiring international mediation efforts led by

President Bongo with the joint United Nations/OAU Special Envoy, Mr. Sahnoun.

21. Despite the setback in Brazzaville and persistent tensions in the Great Lakes region and in a number of other Central African States, I applaud the efforts of Central African States to find peaceful solutions to their region's crises and to strengthen both internal and inter-State harmony on the basis of good governance, the rule of law and mutual respect. While outside assistance can help, there is no substitute for determined action by those most directly concerned.

22. The activities of the Standing Advisory Committee in 1997 demonstrated once again the value of having such a mechanism. The agreements reached by Committee members to set up a subregional early warning mechanism, to control the illicit trade in arms and drugs, to retrain demobilized troops for civilian life and to enhance the capacity of Central African States to participate more effectively in future peace missions in the area would, if implemented, contribute significantly to continuing efforts to end the scourge of violence, destruction and suffering in the subregion. I also welcome the growing attention that those countries are paying to issues of participatory democracy and respect for human rights and the rule of law as part of a strategy for durable peace.

23. The General Assembly has, from the outset, strongly supported the Committee's efforts. The Committee is a forum for dialogue and confidence-building in an extremely volatile area. It has shown a great sense of responsibility and seriousness in the manner in which it has handled sensitive and delicate issues and challenges. It should continue to receive the support and encouragement of the international community. I appeal, in this connection, to member States and the international community as a whole to contribute generously to the United Nations

Trust Fund set up to help implement the Committee's programme of work. It would be sad indeed if the important confidence-building measures agreed by the Committee were to be left unimplemented because of lack of funds.

"I deeply regret the build-up of stocks of weapons in the central African subregion. While military spending has fallen significantly in all continents, this trend is not necessarily reflected in a uniform reduction nor does it apply to all types of weapons.

I personally am deeply concerned at the growing and often illicit arms traffic in the subregion, especially of small arms."

Kofi A. Annan
Secretary-General of the United Nations
7 July 1997

Statements of the Secretary-General
dealing with the UN Standing Advisory Committee on Security Questions in Central Africa

Statement on behalf of Secretary-General Boutros Boutros-Ghali at the Organizational Meeting of the UN Standing Advisory Committee on Security Questions in Central Africa
Yaounde, Cameroon, 27-31 July 1992
(Original statement in English)

(Delivered by his representative Mr. Prvoslav Davinic, Director, Office for Disarmament Affairs)

Permit me from the outset, to convey to you the best wishes of the Secretary-General of the United Nations, Dr. Boutros Boutros-Ghali, for the success of this historic gathering.

Not only in his formal position as Head of an organization in charge of maintaining international peace and security but also as a son of this great Continent, the Secretary-General strongly applauds and supports recent initiatives by the Governments of the Member States of the Economic Community of Central African States (ECCAS), to rid this part of the Continent of the scourge of conflict and to lay a viable foundation for sustainable security, stability and development. It was therefore with great pleasure and satisfaction that the Secretary-General, in response to General Assembly resolution 46/37B endorsed by all Member States, established recently under the auspices of the United Nations the Standing Advisory Committee on Security Questions in Central Africa. We are meeting here today to inaugurate the work of this auspicious body.

I would like, in this connexion, to express my deep gratitude and appreciation to the Government and People of the Republic of Cameroon, under the leadership of H.E. President Paul Biya, for kindly agreeing to host this meeting in their friendly capital, Yaounde, and for the warm and generous welcome they have extended to all of us since our arrival in this beautiful country. By holding `this organizational session of the Standing Advisory Committee in Cameroon, we are also paying a most fitting tribute to its Government for the strong support it gave to this idea and for the leadership it provided over the years in the United Nations for the efforts leading to the adoption of resolution 46/37B of 6 December 1991. I cannot fail to acknowledge the most important role which you Mr. Chairman, in your capacity as the Minister for External Relations of Cameroon, played in bringing about a successful realization of this endeavor of crucial significance. It is highly appreciated.

Due acknowledgment must also be given to the Government of Gabon, represented here by H.E. Martin-Fidèle Magnaga, Minister for National Defense, Security and Immigration. Gabon has from the outset persistently and with great determination lent its support to the efforts of Central African States to make this initiative come true.

It is, indeed, all the Member States of the Economic Community of Central African States which deserve appreciation and admiration of the international community for the visionary decision to join forces in establishing a mechanism for channeling efforts to create more peaceful and secure conditions for their existence and further development. It is a challenging task, but the one which will bring enormous benefits to all.

This meeting is taking place under particularly auspicious circumstances. The world is undergoing momentous, indeed historic changes. As the twentieth century comes to a close, the international community approaches the new millennium with more reasons for hope in the attainability of a safer world than at any other period in the past half century.

The cold war is over. East/West relations, and especially the relationship between the two most powerful nuclear-weapon states, the United States and Russia, have undergone dramatic changes. No longer do these nations confront each other as enemies; they now reach out to each other as partners in the rebuilding of a world scarred by decades of mistrust, misplaced priorities and needless death and destruction.

The great changes taking place in the political scenario are marked, however, by uniquely contradictory trends. As the two major nuclear powers continue to negotiate arms reduction agreements and the countries of Europe are eliminating enormous quantities of weapons and reducing armed forces, the proliferation of weapons of mass destruction threatens to increase, and conventional arms continue to be amassed in many parts of the world.

Furthermore, the easing of tensions between East and West has unveiled other kind of conflicts and new types of problems. Fierce new assertions of nationalism and sovereignty have sprung up, and the cohesion of States is threatened by brutal ethnic, religious, social, cultural or linguistic strife. As racism becomes recognized for the destructive force it is and as apartheid is being dismantled, new racial tensions are rising and finding expression in violence. Poverty, disease, famine, oppression and despair abound, joining to produce millions of refugees and displaced persons, as well as massive migrations of peoples within and beyond national borders.

In Africa itself, there has unfortunately been a steady and alarming decline in the quality of life since the 1980's. African economies, already the weakest and most fragile in the world, are further undermined by continuing civil strife in many parts of the region. Many millions of Africans have been lost to war and famine. Many more are stunted by disease and ignorance. Widespread hopelessness could soon drift into debilitating despair, dooming this proud and richly endowed Continent to a future without dignity, unless effective measures and policies are put into place to change not only the ways things are done but, above all, the attitudes that condition and dictate human reactions and official policies.

Among the causes of Africa's economic stagnation, perhaps the most devastating have been the countless incidents of armed conflict and civil strife that have ravaged African society since the independence era opened over thirty years ago. Some data show that in the past three decades, wars have claimed about seven million African lives, either directly or indirectly. The region's infrastructure has been damaged or destroyed in affected areas, millions of Africans have been driven into refugee camps in neighbouring countries, the brain drain has escalated and military budgets have risen sharply, diverting already limited resources that could have gone to support socio-economic programmes.

There is little doubt that war hampers development and progress, breeds mistrust and tension and encourages wasteful military spending. Yet, wars and conflict continue. To reverse this trend decisively and effectively is a challenge that no one nation, no matter how powerful, can carry out alone. The successful realization of this task requires concerted international action and a new spirit among nations everywhere to forswear war as an option or as an instrument of policy.

The initiative you have taken, aimed at

realizing confidence-building measures and measures to promote common security and development in Central Africa, is a major step in the right direction. Pursued to its logical conclusion, this process of finding regional solutions to regional problems, could result in a stable and integrated community where inter-state boundaries would be seen as bridges of friendship, solidarity and cooperation rather than as zones of conflict and separation.

If the goal we all seek in this endeavor is a stable peace where security and progress can flourish for the benefit of the tens of millions of people living in this part of Africa, then we should conceive a concrete strategy that identifies specific measures to be pursued towards that end. That task is the primary responsibility of the Governments of the Central African States themselves. Nevertheless, it is possible to carve out a number of broad areas within the overall framework of which the pursuit of peace offers wide possibilities for progress. These include arms limitation and disarmament, preventive diplomacy, peace-making, peace-keeping and peace-building, including confidence building.

A commitment by all countries concerned to arms restraint and to the pursuit of security at the lowest possible level of armaments and armed forces would certainly contribute to confidence-building among States. So would collateral measures of openness and transparency by States in their military affairs. The decision by the General Assembly to establish an international register of conventional arms is seen as an important instrument in this direction. If all the countries in a specific region were to participate in such a programme aimed at making their military transactions more open and public, this could facilitate collective efforts of arms control helping eliminate the mistrust and suspicion on which the arms race and armed conflict feed.

Since the arms race feeds on inter-state tensions and conflict, preventive diplomacy, which seeks to resolve disputes before they degenerate into violence, emerges as another essential element in the pursuit of a stable and secure peace. If, despite all attempts at prevention armed confrontation should still break out, peace-making and peace-keeping measures can be envisaged to halt the conflict and to bring the adversaries to the negotiating table. Peace-making and peace-keeping also enhance opportunities for long-term peace-building and confidence-building by helping to preserve the recurrence of armed hostilities and by engaging the parties in the search for solutions to the disputes between them through peaceful means.

Each of these areas of action has intrinsic value of its own. Taken together, and implemented comprehensively and in an integrated manner by the countries concerned, they offer perhaps the surest avenue towards genuine peace and harmony among nations.

It is often easy as we focus on the numerous problems confronting Africa, to lose sight of the many positive developments taking place in the region. I am particularly struck by the deep and resilient spirit of compassion and hope that is felt across the Continent. Even as they face massive difficulties of their own, African countries have kept their doors open to their less fortunate neighbours fleeing wars, persecution and natural disasters. And, even when the future appears bleakest, the peoples of the region refuse to despair. Free at last from the ideological distortions of the Cold War and endowed with an enduring spirit of human solidarity and creativity, Africa has now a renewed opportunity not only to get back on its feet, but indeed to grow and prosper. The march towards democratization and respect of human rights is opening up the political systems and making leaders more accountable and more responsive to popular concerns. An enabling environment for stability and economic progress is being built. There are still risks, and there are no guarantees that the present encouraging trend cannot be reversed. But, with initiatives such as the one we are here to launch, the countries of the region seem to be demonstrating a strong determination not only to persevere with the reforms but above all to push forward even more. With the recognition that failure this time could be truly catastrophic for Africa's future, progress is not only feasible, it is indeed attainable.

In this context, I would like to pay tribute to all the member States of the Economic Community of Central African States for the wisdom and vision they have long shown in pursuing constructive measures of confidence-building and cooperation rather than destructive policies of inter-state conflict and rivalry based on narrow national self interest. By closely associating the United Nations with their efforts, the States of the sub-region of Central Africa have demonstrated a complementary commitment to African solidarity and self-reliance as well as to international co-operation, within the framework of the United Nations. Not only does such wisdom and realism augur well for the future work of the Standing Advisory Committee, it also enhances the prospects and lays the foundations of sub- regional peace, progress and integration in this important part of Africa.

I can assure you of the continued support of the United Nations Secretariat for the attainment of the positive objectives you seek. The Secretariat and in particular the Office for Disarmament Affairs stand ready to contribute to the success of these initiatives. As an expression of the utmost importance which we attach to your efforts, the Secretary-General has appointed as the Secretary of this Committee one of the most capable senior officers of the Office for Disarmament Affairs, Mr. Sammy Kum Buo. I am confident that Mr. Buo will serve you

well and with utmost devotion and dedication.

I wish you success in the important task ahead of you.

Statement on behalf of Secretary-General Boutros Boutros-Ghali at the Third Ministerial Meeting of the UN Standing Advisory Committee on Security Questions in Central Africa
Libreville, Gabon
30 August - 3 September 1993
(Original statement in French)

(Delivered by his representative Mr. Hassen Fodha, Director, UN Information Centre, Paris)

On behalf of the Secretary-General of the United Nations, Dr. Boutros Boutros-Ghali, I am pleased and honoured to convey to all of you his best wishes as I welcome you most heartily to the second meeting of the United Nations Standing Advisory Committee on Security Questions in Central Africa for 1993.

Allow me, first of all, to pay a most deserved tribute to the people and Government of Gabon under the leadership of President Omar Bongo for agreeing to host this very important meeting in their beautiful capital city of Libreville, for their hospitality and friendship which are auspicious assets to our meeting, and most importantly too, for their sustained efforts in the preservation of durable peace and security in the subregion and on the continent as a whole. Still fresh in our minds is Gabon's key role as facilitator in the peaceful settlement of the political deadlock in Congo that not-so-long ago threatened the security and unity of that friendly and neighbouring country. The peace talks happened here, in this very city of Libreville, barely one month ago. This, indeed, was a commendable role that falls within the gambit of what our budding committee is all about. The government of Gabon has actively been involved, too, in the original process that paved the way for the creation of this committee ever since one of this country's eminent sons, General Idriss Ngari was elected Chairman of the Conference on confidence-building, security and development within the Economic Community of Central African States in February 1988.

I wish to pay a well deserved homage too, to all the eleven countries of this subregion for their foresightedness and vision in initiating the creation of this Committee and for their continued investment of efforts in the realization of its work programme. By this, you have all earned the admiration and encouragement of the international community. Indeed, what you have begun here is one of the important realizations in the recent history of inter-national relations: you have all agreed to unite your efforts and political wills in achieving durable peace, security and progress by building confidence, maximizing dialogue and resolving peacefully, differences among the great peoples that you are. The United Nations watches with pride, each step of your commendable work. From Yaounde to Bujumbura, and today in Libreville, the programme of work and the meetings of the Committee are eloquent testimony of your determination to achieve the best result. I have no doubts that your untiring spirit, together with the resilience, the drive and the enthusiasm which is your hallmark in this subregion has inspired the work of the distinguished experts who have been meeting since three days ago, and will carry our work through to fruition.

Allow me, therefore, distinguished experts to commend you for your hard work and high sense of responsibility which you continue to show in the furtherance of peace and security in this subregion in particular. You constitute, indeed, the lifeblood of the Standing Advisory Committee on Security Questions in Central Africa.

Allow me also, to recognize, on behalf of the United Nations, the role played by the Economic Community of Central African States (ECCAS) in the reconstruction of this subregion. ECCAS does not only constitute a vehicle through which the vast economic and human resources can be transformed into a sustainable base for durable progress and social well-being for all, as a sub-regional organization, it constitutes also, a viable medium for building confidence among its members. In this regard, the functional relationship between ECCAS and the Standing Advisory Committee on Security Questions in Central Africa cannot be underestimated. It is therefore with regret that I note the difficulties which ECCAS is presently experiencing particularly at a time when its services are needed more than ever before in an increasingly economic hard pressed subregion. It's revitalization would certainly put the subregion back on the rails of development and social progress.

We must not loose sight of the horrors currently plaguing our world. The upsurge of tribal wars in Europe and elsewhere tragically vivified in particular by the on-going war in Bosnia and Herzegovina have unfortunately increased the post-cold war challenges for the international community and the United Nations in particular at a time when the resources of the world organization have been stretched thin. Sub-regional initiatives such as the Standing Advisory Committee are therefore encouraged and are indeed, vitally complementary in the realization of the Secretary-General's new vision for world peace. On board the Standing Advisory Committee, let us move out of the shadows of the horrors of wars and hatred towards a permanent springtime of hope and progress.

In Africa, an unfortunate depressing combination of political upheavals largely orchestrated by a reluctance in the implementation of the democratic processes and economic hardships, has severely compromised the quality of life and dampened hopes for the future. In Angola, Liberia, Somalia, South Africa and the Sudan most notably, millions of Africans are lost to meaningless internecine conflicts; and many more are forced to wander hopelessly as refugees, away from loved ones and their fatherlands. And while many parts of the world move forward and with resolve to better times, many countries in Africa, are regressing, falling down the precipice of despair.

African economies, already the weakest and most fragile in the world, are indeed further undermined by the continuing civil strife. The armed conflicts have destroyed infrastructure and depleted human resources. Instead, what has remained steady have been rising military budgets, perversely diverting limited resources that could have gone to support socio-economic programmes.

It is evident that war and conflicts hamper development and progress and breed hatred, tensions and wasteful expenditure in the purchasing of military supplies. We have all watched, helpless, how some of the countries of the continent have continued to slide into anarchy, breaking up into murderous factions, killing and maiming psychologically and physically their human capital. Of course, no business concern would want to invest in such countries where capital is not protected, where markets can not strive. In economic terms, this state of affairs makes it difficult for Africa to benefit from increased foreign direct investments that economists are predicting for the next years and into the next century.

This depressing picture is not a fixture for eternity. It can be improved upon. To change it, to reverse the trend decisively and effectively is a challenge that can be faced if the will and the good faith are there. But it is a challenge that no one nation, no matter how powerful, can face alone. It is a daunting task to rebuild when the resources have been squandered. Many hands do lighter work, and the successful realization of this task requires concerted action and a determination by all to stop resorting to war as an option or as an instrument of policy either at the domestic or at the inter-state level.

In the midst of this climate of pervading despair, you, the peoples of the central African subregion have shown that all is not lost, that <u>a solid crisis-and conflict-free common home</u> can be built here. The encouraging developments in the peace processes and reconciliation in Rwanda, Congo and Chad are noteworthy in this regard. The protracted armed conflict in Angola and the already too-long political and social stalemate in Zaire seriously retard global human and economic development in the subregion and should compel a concerted political action by the govern-ments of the subregion. On behalf of the Secretary-General, I wish to commend those governments who have already lent their support to his personal representative in Angola in his on-going efforts to galvanize the necessary subregional supports in the resolution of the Angolan conflict.

A frank pursuit of the implementation of the democratic processes underway in many countries and a commitment by all governments to arms restraint and to the attainment of security by the lowest possible level of armaments and armed forces will certainly contribute to enhancing stability in the subregion. On the other hand measures of openness and transparency by states in their military affairs would promote confidence among states in the region.

Here in Libreville, you have begun deepening reflection on the best ways and means of realizing this climate of stability, confidence and trust in the subregion.

Indeed, noteworthy among the tasks of the experts, have been the finalization of the non-aggression pact among member states; the elaboration of specific measures to promote the balanced and gradual reduction of armed forces, armaments and military budgets; the consideration of specific measures and mechanisms for crisis management and peacekeeping in the subregion, as well as a review of the geopolitical and security-related developments in the subregion, which have included the situations in Angola, Rwanda and Zaire. This has been a very useful agenda which, if translated into positive political action would go a long way in stabilizing this subregion. I have no doubt that the ministers and heads of delegations here gathered, will construe to the work of the experts the required political action.

I wish all of you good luck and success in the completion of your work.

Statement on behalf of Secretary-General Boutros Boutros-Ghali at the Fourth Ministerial Meeting of the UN Standing Advisory Committee on Security Questions in Central Africa
Yaounde, Cameroon, 4-8 April 1994
(Original statement in French)

(Delivered by his representative Mr. Herbert M'Cleod, UN Resident Coordinator, Yaounde)
The Secretary-General was dismayed to learn of the deaths of the Presidents of Burundi and Rwanda, and has sent messages of condolence to the families and peoples of the two countries.

He has instructed me to read out the following message:

On the occasion of this ministerial meeting of the Standing Advisory Committee on Security Questions in Central Africa, I should like, on my own behalf and on behalf of the United Nations, to offer you my fullest encouragement and to wish you every success in your work.

Your Advisory Committee is, in my view, a body of considerable importance. I am convinced that a high-level meeting such as yours can make a major contribution to the restoration and consolidation of peace in your region. Such initiatives offer the best chance of translating the objectives set out in the Charter of the United Nations into reality in States and continents.

Let us never forget that peace and security are prerequisites for the formulation of genuine economic and social development policies. Without peace, no development is possible.

Africa, our continent, which has suffered so greatly from so many ills, must rediscover hope. It would be inadmissible for the women and men of Africa to be denied the right to peace and the right to development that everyone else enjoys.

It is through meetings such as this that these two vital necessities can be assured.

That is why I attach so much importance to this meeting in Yaoundé and so warmly congratulate the Cameroonian authorities for hosting it.

I shall be sure to keep informed of the result of your work. I should like to see all my African brothers working together to put their goodwill and imagination at the service of our continent.

**Message on behalf of
Secretary-General Boutros Boutros-Ghali
at the Sixth Ministerial Meeting of the UN
Standing Advisory Committee on
Security Questions in Central Africa**
Brazzaville, Congo, 20-24 March 1995
(Original statement in French)

**(Delivered by his representative
Mr. Wilfred de Souza, Director, Africa
Division, Department of Political Affairs)**

As you begin your work, I should like, on my own behalf and on behalf of the United Nations, to offer you my strongest encouragement. Believe me, this is not purely formal encouragement. It is, on the contrary, the expression both of my hopes and of my concern.

Indeed, I regard such a meeting as an expression of the determination of your States to deal with the crucial question of security in your region. This seems to me all the more important in that we all have in mind the tragedies which central Africa has witnessed recently and the serious threats which still hang over it. It is therefore essential that Africans should learn to draw upon their own resources, their ancient civilization, their deeply rooted culture and their ancestral wisdom to find the means to take charge of their own collective destiny.

Your meeting is indeed the proof of this determination. More than ever, it is essential that the African States should take steps to find ways whereby they themselves can maintain peace and security on the continental, the subcontinental and, above all, the regional level. This security calls for the improvements of measures designed to build confidence between States. It also calls for the use of effective preventive diplomacy designed, inter alia, to prevent tragedies of the kind we have witnessed.

It also entails an African disarmament policy, and to this end it is essential that urgent measures should be taken. For it is important simultaneously to ensure well planned disarmament and to prevent arms proliferation on our continent.

There are moments in history when each must feel that he has the responsibility for his own destiny. This is the case with you today. And you would be missing this great rendezvous with history if you did not give yourselves the means to ensure the security of your region.

I have confidence in you. You have the support of the United Nations and of the international community as a whole. I am sure that you will prove worthy of the hopes which we place in you.

The security of central Africa is today a categorical imperative. For this reason the States gathered here today must demonstrate a spirit of responsibility and a great deal of imagination. The maintenance of peace and the guaranteeing of security in central Africa are prerequisites for sustainable development in the region. But the States of central Africa can also thereby set an example to the continent as a whole.

My dear brothers and sisters, I wish you all success in your work. Rest assured that I shall follow with great interest the outcome of your important meeting.

Message on behalf of Secretary-General Boutros Boutros-Ghali at the Seventh Ministerial Meeting of the UN Standing Advisory Committee on Security Questions in Central Africa
Brazzaville, Congo
28 August - 1 September 1995
(Original statement in French)

(Delivered by his representative Mr. Alioune Blondin Beye, Special Representative of the Secretary-General in Angola)

This meeting of the United Nations Standing Advisory Committee on Security Questions in Central Africa is being held at a time when the subregion is witnessing events that are crucial to its destiny.

Although some situations have taken a turn for the better, unfortunately the same cannot be said of many others.

The recent meeting in Franceville, on 10 August, between the two Angolan leaders, President Eduardo dos Santos and Dr. Jonas Savimbi, under the auspices of the President of the Gabonese Republic, His Excellency El Hadj Oman Bongo, confirmed all the hopes raised three months earlier, on 6 May in Lusaka, when the Angolan peace process entered a new phase.

The United Nations is heartened to note that the Angolans have embarked resolutely on the path leading to a lasting peace based on national reconciliation, democracy and economic and social development, as well as respect for the rights and fundamental freedoms of the individual.

The United Nations strongly encourages the Angolan Government to step up its efforts to establish the conditions necessary for the rapid return to barracks of forces of the National Union for the Total Independence of Angola (UNITA), now that United Nations battalions are about to begin the final phase of their deployment throughout Angolan territory.

Now more than ever, it is necessary to maintain the momentum that was generated first in Lusaka and then in Franceville, and to translate it into specific and decisive actions to satisfy the hopes of the Angolan population, by restoring a definitive climate of peace for the benefit of all the countries in the subregion.

The United Nations supports and is following with great interest the preparations for the forthcoming round-table meeting of donors for Angola, which is due to be held next month in Brussels. We earnestly hope that the international community will, once again, size up the situation correctly and respond forcefully, as it has often done in the past, to the expectations of the suffering populations who need international assistance in order to kick-start an economy that is, potentially, one of the most promising in Africa.

Another satisfaction can be found in the outcome of recent events in Sao Tome and Principe. The active mediation of some countries from the subregion led, happily, to the restoration of republican legality in that country, to our great relief. The example given shows the need for solidarity among - and the interdependence of - the countries of the subregion; their show of solidarity, based on ongoing dialogue and mutual aid, is today totally justified and confirmed.

On the other hand, in another part of your vast subregion, the international community can but stress its concern at the tragedy befalling hundreds of thousands of Rwandan refugees. Recent developments in eastern Zaire, on the border with Rwanda, require, in the first place, the attention of your respective Governments, for these events call into question the great humanitarian principles that all States are duty-bound to observe at all times.

The United Nations urges the

Governments of Zaire, Rwanda and Burundi to take urgent steps to put an end to the great hardships endured by those thousands of refugees, the majority of whom are women and children suffering from diseases, malnutrition and violence of all kinds.

Everyone is aware of the serious risk to security and stability in the subregion posed by these displaced populations in the grip of panic and despair. It is up to the States to create the conditions to encourage those of their citizens who, for various reasons, have left the country to return and settle down again in their own land.

Not only must they, as States Members of the United Nations, respect the principles of international humanitarian law, but they also have a moral obligation to receive and shelter foreign populations displaced from their place of origin by wars, famines, epidemics or any other catastrophe, whether it be natural or man-made. The international community has a duty to help countries to bear the burden of such a presence on their soil.

In this regard, the United Nations pays tribute to the tremendous sacrifices made by some countries in the subregion in sheltering for a relatively long period hundreds of thousands of refugees who left their countries for various reasons.

We urge these receiving countries to continue to extend their hospitality, and we assure them that the international community will spare no efforts to help these refugees return as soon as possible to their country of origin.

We should always remember that in situations of conflict, the first victims of which are the most vulnerable sectors of society, hasty solutions almost always lead to even more intractable situations which endanger the already precarious security situation in the regions concerned. We then witness large-scale violations of human rights and this gives rise to a widespread feeling of insecurity throughout the subregion.

That is why the Security Council regularly draws the attention of States to the need to respect the rights and freedoms of individuals under all circumstances, and to ensure that these rights and freedoms are respected. It is also why there is a special human rights unit in every peacekeeping operation.

We are confident that your respective Governments will continue to take particular care in this matter.

The international community will continue to monitor closely the security situation in Central Africa, particularly in areas where sources of tension still exist - Rwanda, Burundi and Angola - that might spread to all the States in the subregion.

The laudable efforts of the various Governments concerned or involved should not lead us to downplay the often considerable risks of reopening situations which have been stabilized or aggravating underlying tensions that may seem to have been brought under control.

The United Nations will pursue, with all the means at its disposal, the actions under way, and remains convinced that your respective Governments will be able to correctly assess what is really at stake at any given time, without losing sight of the legitimate concerns of contributing countries and organizations, desirous above all of ensuring that the considerable resources devoted to the region's security and stabilization channeled increasingly towards the development of the immense economic and human potential of this region of Africa.

I wish you much success in your work!

**Statement on behalf of
Secretary-General Boutros Boutros-Ghali
at the Eighth Ministerial Meeting of the
UN Standing Advisory Committee on
Security Questions in Central Africa**
Yaounde, Cameroon, 15-19 April 1996
(Original statement in English)

**(Delivered by his representative
Mr. Prvoslav Davinic, Director, Centre for
Disarmament Affairs)**

Please allow me to begin with a
well-deserved tribute to the Government
and people of Cameroon.

Once again, Cameroon is welcoming the
Standing Advisory Committee on Security
Questions in Central Africa and providing it
with wonderful working conditions and
facilities. Cameroon's consistent and
generous support for the Committee
testifies to its traditional hospitality and
strong sense of solidarity with Africa, and
with the world. This same solidarity shows
brilliantly in Cameroon's steadfast support
for the United Nations and its work.

On behalf of the United Nations, I
express my deep appreciation to the
Government and people of Cameroon. The
open and cooperative atmosphere they
have created augurs well for the objectives
sought for Central Africa by this Committee.

Today, you meet in Yaounde to tackle an
issue of vital importance -- how to avert
further conflict within and between the
States of Central Africa and to promote
confidence-building measures. Against the
background of recent convulsions in this
subregion, no endeavour is more important
nor more urgent than this mission to close
the chapter of violence which has so
polarized and traumatized the people of
Central Africa for so long.

We have entered a period in world
history in which most conflicts occur not
across, but within State borders. Most are

unlikely to motivate the international
community to create, in response, a force
such as that deployed by the North Atlantic
Treaty Organization (NATO) and its partners
in Bosnia. In any one case, the national
interest of any one State or group of States
may not seem directly affected. But all
States have a strong interest in preventing a
global pattern of violence, in checking the
disease of conflict, and in deterring
would-be aggressors.

Your efforts, therefore, are important not
only to Central Africa. Peace and security in
Central Africa is integral to peace and
security in the Africa region, which is integral
to peace and security in the world as a
whole. And so today, as you, the
representatives of every country in Central
Africa, endeavour to prevent further and
future tragedy in your subregion, the entire
international community is with you.

Barely four months ago, the fiftieth
session of the United Nations General
Assembly reaffirmed its backing for your
efforts. In its resolution 50/71B, adopted on
12 December 1995, the Assembly called for
wide international support to facilitate the full
implementation of your programme of work.
And last month, as requested by the
Assembly, I established a United Nations
trust fund to raise, through voluntary
contributions, additional resources to
support your work. I am encouraged by the
interest in and response to my appeal thus
far, both from within and outside the Africa
region. Here in Yaounde I want especially
to thank those governments which have
already contributed. And I appeal to all
governments for additional and continued
support.

At the same time, I wish to reaffirm my
strong personal support for the efforts of this
Committee. Your determination,
perseverance and commitment to peace are
an example for all, as is the wisdom of the
course you have chosen. As underscored
by the high toll taken by conflicts in Central

Africa and elsewhere, in both human and financial terms, and in the high cost of peace-keeping, humanitarian relief and reconstruction, preventive action makes good sense.

Today, your Committee opens its eighth ministerial session. In four years of effort, you have reached agreements on complex and sensitive issues. This is no small achievement. The next step must be implementation. Unless implemented, these agreements will diminish in value, and I fear that the credibility of the Committee itself will be damaged and its objectives undermined. Therefore, I join the General Assembly in expressing the hope that your governments will prove to the world their political will and sign, in the near future, the Non-Aggression Pact, initialed in this very building nearly a year and a half ago.

I also join the General Assembly in commending the decision recently taken by your governments, within the framework of this Committee, to designate units in their respective armed forces for possible peace assignments under the auspices of the United Nations or the Organization of African Unity (OAU). This measure has potentially far-reaching implications for conflict-management prospects in Central Africa. Had such a measure been enacted two years ago, a massive human tragedy could have been averted in Rwanda. If fully implemented, your decision will help prevent another such tragedy in the future.

Full implementation would be a concrete and responsible development, promoting mutual confidence among participating member States and enhancing the credibility and effectiveness of this Committee. The General Assembly's appeal for voluntary contributions to facilitate the training of these peace units, once designated, deserves the widest possible support in order to ensure that the units will be prepared and readied for deployment on short notice, should the need arise.

The Non-Aggression Pact and the designated peace units can provide a solid foundation upon which this Committee's future efforts can be built. Let me look, then, at the road ahead of you, and at some specific measures which may be required.

First, the deadly frequency of armed conflict in Central Africa clearly calls for a commitment on the part of all concerned to make every effort to resolve disputes by peaceful means. Diplomacy cannot work miracles, especially when one party to a dispute believes it stands to gain from resorting to force. But all too often military action has been initiated before all possible diplomatic options have been exhausted. I ask you today to reaffirm your commitment under and in the spirit of Article 33 of the United Nations Charter to explore and pursue all possible peaceful means to prevent armed conflict and the outbreak of war. These include but are not confined to negotiation, enquiry, mediation, conciliation, arbitration, judicial settlement, diplomatic persuasion and pressure, and resorting to regional agencies or arrangements.

At the subregional level, preventive diplomacy can be particularly productive. Hence, the special significance of your ongoing efforts. As neighbours, your countries not only are aware of and often affected by each other's problems, but you may also face the same problems. You may, therefore, be more alert, capable and motivated to act to prevent trouble in your neighbourhood. With your periodic meetings to review the geo-political situation in Central Africa, you can facilitate the identification of potential trouble spots where preventive diplomacy may need to be employed. You can contribute to strengthening mutual trust and cooperation among your respective countries.

Your efforts will be complemented and supported by preventive diplomacy at the regional and global levels. At the regional level, the OAU is now building an effective early-warning capability to enable it to act in a timely and effective manner to prevent disputes from escalating into full-blown conflicts. I continue to seek closer and improved cooperation with the OAU and various other regional organizations and arrangements, especially in the areas of peace-making, peace-keeping and preventive diplomacy. These can be an essential complement to United Nations efforts at the global level to keep watch over points of possible danger and prepare the international community to move decisively when needed.

Preventive diplomacy, however, is a concept not limited to diplomatic efforts alone. Effective preventive diplomacy may, in some cases, require preventive deployment. In all cases, the many activities commonly associated with post-conflict peace-building can be an important component of preventive diplomacy. In this context, I wish to draw your attention to what I have termed "micro-disarmament" -- action to control and reduce the production, transfer and stockpiling of conventional small arms and light weapons, which are responsible for most of the deaths in today's conflicts. The uncontrolled proliferation of such weapons is itself a cause of suspicion, tension and even war, most often in the poorest countries of the world. I have, on several occasions, called for the eradication of the illicit trade in these weapons and for micro-disarmament to be understood and pursued in the wider context of preventive diplomacy and peace-building.

Both developed and developing countries have a major role to play in promoting micro-disarmament. Richer countries manufacture and sell the weapons to poorer countries at a healthy profit. The poorer countries not only loose scarce revenue to arms acquisition, but also frequently fall victim to these imported instruments of violence. The same wealthy States then spend much greater sums on emergency relief for the victims of the wars their arms made possible. This senseless trend must be reversed. I reiterate my appeal to all producers and recipients to show restraint in the interest of saving human lives, especially in areas of the world, such as yours, which have already suffered so much for so long from the negative consequences of the arms flow.

On a similar note, I reiterate my call for a comprehensive international ban on the production, stockpiling, trade and use of all anti-personnel land-mines and mine components. You in Central Africa are well aware of the terrible toll taken by land-mines on innocent lives, the heavy burden of care for land-mine victims on developing societies, and the formidable obstacles land-mines pose to post-conflict reconstruction and development.

These peace-building activities make startlingly clear the fundamental link between efforts, such as yours, to prevent, control and resolve conflicts, and efforts to advance long-term economic and social development. Central Africa is richly endowed with natural and human resources. Its people are dynamic and enterprising. Yet, a destructive legacy of conflicts in the area has hampered development. And the lack of development has fueled still more conflict. Efforts such as yours to build mutual confidence and shared security will be central, indeed indispensable, to the effort to turn the rich potential of Central Africa into the prosperity and freedom its countries and peoples seek and deserve. And, at the same time, the prosperity and freedom achieved through progress in development and democratization will, in the long run, prove to be the most effective and lasting form of preventive diplomacy.

Thus, your peace efforts in Central Africa are inextricably linked to development efforts in Central Africa, and to the peace and development of the African continent as a whole. Clearly, there is a need for a comprehensive approach to be applied at the national, subregional, regional and international levels.

The new and unprecedented system-wide United Nations Special Initiative for Africa embodies just such a comprehensive approach. This multi-billion dollar programme is the most significant and largest coordinated action to date to mobilize international support for Africa's priority development goals, especially in the areas of health and education. It represents the first time that the United Nations system has launched such an initiative to support the development aspirations of the people of an entire region. And it is designed to do so in a way that takes into account the interlinked nature of Africa's most critical challenges.

The United-Nations estimates that prospects for Africa's economic recovery are currently brighter and greater than they have been in recent years. Our new system-wide Special Initiative aims to build on that momentum and to promote mutually reinforcing advances in peace and development. The success of your ongoing efforts in this Committee to rebuild Central Africa will be indispensable to these objectives.

The challenges you face are significant. The United Nations and the international community will stand by you for as long as you persist in your determination to succeed. I wish you every success in your deliberations and in the critical tasks that lie ahead.

Statement by Secretary-General Boutros Boutros-Ghali on the occasion of the First Summit Meeting of Heads of State and Government of Member States of the UN Standing Advisory Committee on Security Questions in Central Africa
Yaounde, Cameroon, 8 July 1996
(Original statement in French)

I should like to begin by telling you how happy I am to be among you again today, on the occasion of the session of the Standing Advisory Committee. I attach the greatest importance to your institution and your work.

Since 1992, I have had several opportunities to stress what an essential role you are playing in helping to bring peace to a region whose difficulties and uncertainties are familiar to us all.

We all know that security in Central Africa must be guaranteed. Once again, I should like to say that I have confidence In your wisdom and In your sense of responsibility.

I therefore welcome this first meeting among Heads of State and Government. It Is a sign of your commitment to take charge of the problems of Africa, not only at the continental level, but also at this regional and subregional levels.

The goal of security being pursued by your Committee leads you, quite naturally, to place emphasis on the peaceful settlement of disputes among States.

It Is in that context that I wish to commend the efforts of His Excellency Mr. Desti-Arsene Tsaty-Boungou in working towards the preparation of a non-aggression pact.

I also wish to encourage you In your efforts to link the imperative of security with the objective of disarmament.

In this connection, I wish to reiterate the importance of what I have referred to as micro-disarmament, for it is essential to the normalization of living conditions on the African continent and to the reconstruction of the war-affected countries.

I therefore wish to reaffirm, before you, that the United Nations is ready to support the programme of regional micro-disarmament which you are now preparing.

The proliferation of small arms on the African continent must be curbed: greater transparency in the acquisition of armaments is indispensable, stricter controls over illegal transfers of all types of weapons are urgently needed.

In all of those areas, you can rely on the collaboration of the United Nations.

But this security and disarmament goal must also be followed up both by short-term and by long-term measures.

In the short term, we must emphasize conflict-prevention mechanisms and mechanisms to ensure that action is taken as promptly as possible, before a conflict breaks out, before it spreads, before it degenerates.

I fully share your concerns regarding the establishment of early-warning mechanisms. Since 1993, the Organization of African Unity has stressed the importance of such procedures throughout the continent. I am gratified that the same spirit is urging you to implement such procedures throughout your region. I can only encourage you in your initiative.

But we must also be aware that the security of Central Africa can be assured in a lasting and permanent manner only through long-term measures, first and foremost, the promotion of democracy and the establishment of the rule of law.

I know fully well that you are concerned about that situation and are responsive to that goal. There again, I can tell you that the United Nations will fully support your efforts, for example, with regard to the subregional conference on democratic institutions and peace, for which you have already made plans.

It is through the spirit of democracy that the virtues of tolerance and respect for diversity will become embodied in the various populations. We all know that those are values which the women and men of Africa adhere to. They must therefore be given the institutions that will enable them to affirm and practice those values.

Likewise, the rule of law must be established everywhere, public freedoms must be respected everywhere, and national institutions, such as the army or the police, must act on behalf of all within the framework of democracy everywhere.

I have therefore come here to express my personal solidarity and demonstrate support from the United Nations.

A United Nations fund has been established in support of your endeavours. I am indefatigable in urging donor States to contribute as generously as possible. The United Nations is here to place its resources at the service of your objectives, to the extent possible.

We must work together, and without respite, so that despite the difficulties and the obstacles, the spirit of peace and security might prevail in Central Africa.

To that end, you know you can count fully on me.

Statement on behalf of Secretary-General Boutros Boutros-Ghali on the occasion of the Second Summit Meeting of Heads of State and Government of Member States of the UN Standing Advisory Committee on Security Questions in Central Africa held in an extraordinary context

Brazzaville, Congo, 2-3 December 1996
(Original statement in French)

(Delivered by his representative Mr. Alioune Blondin Beye, Special Representative of the Secretary-General in Angola)

The Secretary-General of the United Nations, your brother Mr. Boutros Boutros-Ghali, has asked me to convey to you his deep regret at not being able to be with you in person, here in Brazzaville, at this special summit of States members of the United Nations Standing Advisory Committee on Security Questions in Central Africa.

It is therefore on his behalf that I have the signal honour to address this illustrious assembly, to convey the international community's deep sense of solidarity in these turbulent and dangerous times for this sensitive region of Africa.

Indeed, this meeting is being held at a time when the situation is particularly worrying, especially in the Great Lakes region, where the continuing deterioration of the situation poses a serious threat to security and stability in the subregion as a whole.

That is why the international community was relieved to learn of this laudable initiative by His Excellency Mr. Pascal Lissouba, President of the Republic of the Congo, and his illustrious peers in the subregion, aware that their primary responsibility is to ensure peace and harmonious coexistence between the sister States and nations of this part of our continent.

This timely reflex of bringing together all the heads of the "great family" in times of crisis or in order to avoid a crisis has its roots in our well- established African traditions commonly known as the "tree of talk", which can certainly be said to have granted its letters patent of nobility to what goes under the term "preventive diplomacy". Your Committee is a favoured instrument of such diplomacy and an ideal forum in which to settle disputes between your respective States and in which to promote relationships of trust between them. That is why the Secretary-General of the United Nations, whom you were pleased to welcome at the first meeting of your Committee at the level of heads of State and Government, on 8 July 1996 in Yaoundé, made a point of reaffirming, on that occasion, the Organization's support for the aims and objectives of your Committee. In this respect, the fact that the Non-Aggression Pact has been signed by practically all States members of the Committee shows the determination that drives the leaders of your subregion and justifies the legitimate hopes of their peoples. It is also reassuring to note that on that occasion the same leaders jointly declared that peace and security in the subregion could only be assured in the long term through respect for human rights, democratization, the establishment of the rule of law and socio-economic development.

The scale of the tensions and the acuteness of the challenges today assailing the subregion of Central Africa are such that not only are the States concerned and the international community as a whole duty-bound to act but they must do so in full knowledge of the urgent need for consultation, solidarity and efficiency.

In Angola, thanks in the first place to the political will of our Angolan brothers (whose Head of State, His Excellency José Eduardo dos Santos, President of the Republic, I am pleased to greet here today), and thanks too to the patient efforts of the international community, the peace process is being consolidated more every day, allowing us today to harbour hopes of a definitive national reconciliation in the fairly near future. However, the current situation in the Great Lakes region, particularly in eastern Zaire, poses a serious threat to international peace and security in this subregion.

The Security Council, in its resolution 1080 (1996) of 15 November, addressed the continuing deterioration in this situation and reminded States of their obligations under the Charter of the United Nations concerning respect for the sovereignty and the territorial integrity of States and for the relevant provisions of international humanitarian law. The Security Council also envisaged a number of measures to confront the crisis, stressing the need for close consultation with the States concerned in the subregion.

There can be no doubt that to give effect to the international community's efforts and initiatives in your subregion requires greater coordination, practical contributions and promptness.

The situation of refugees and displaced persons, despite recent developments which have significantly reduced their numbers, continues to be of major importance for the security of all countries in the region.

That is why your meeting comes at such an opportune time; once again the fate of the peoples of Central Africa lies, quite rightly, in your hands and the initiative for ensuring stability, peace and development in this region is rightly yours.

The international community is listening to you, and intends to fulfil its duty of solidarity towards your peoples. It will be all the more motivated to act since the political will of the States members of your

Committee will be made quite clear at the end of this important meeting. There can be no doubt that you will come up with proposals that will avert the threat of a conflagration the consequences of which cannot be foreseen, and also increase the chances of a just and lasting peace that will benefit all the peoples of Central Africa.

Allow me, Your Excellencies, illustrious guests, to express my heartfelt gratitude for your wonderful, very African hospitality, and for granting me the privilege of a few precious moments of your time to pass on this message from your brother Mr. Boutros Boutros-Ghali, Secretary-General of the United Nations, who sends his sincerest wishes for a successful meeting.

**Message of Secretary-General
Kofi A. Annan
at the Ninth Ministerial Meeting of the UN
Standing Advisory Committee on
Security Questions in Central Africa**
Libreville, Gabon, 7-11 July 1997
(Original statement in French)

**(Delivered by his representative
Mr. Mohamed Sahnoun, UN/OAU Special
Representative for the Great Lakes)**

This Ninth Ministerial Meeting of your Committee is taking place at a particularly critical time in the history of Central Africa. The tragic events of recent months in the Great Lakes region, particularly in the former Zaire, the Central African Republic and Brazzaville, once again demonstrate that the central African subregion continues to be one of the most volatile areas on the African continent.

I can only deeply regret the high cost of these conflicts in terms of human life, suffering, massive movements of refugees and internally displaced persons and the destruction of property and infrastructures in the countries concerned.

At the same time, I am encouraged by the readiness shown by the Governments of the subregion to step up their efforts in the quest for peaceful settlements of the many conflicts there. Your presence here in Libreville is evidence of your determination to work together for security and peace in your region, and I salute the political will which you have shown and encourage you in this endeavour.

The fact that this important meeting is taking place in Libreville also testifies to the essential role played by Gabon in this undertaking. I should like to take this opportunity to pay tribute to President El Hadj Omar Bongo for his tireless efforts to restore peace in the region and his unswerving dedication to the ideals of regional solidarity and cooperation. Let me assure him that he has the support of the United Nations in this endeavour.

Even as you meet, the United Nations is working closely with Central African States in addressing regional security and stability issues.

Efforts are being made to end the political crisis in Brazzaville and intensive moves are under way to consolidate the peace processes in Angola and the Central African Republic.

I am encouraged that calm has now returned to the Democratic Republic of the Congo and I wish to assure you once again that the United Nations is fully committed to working closely with the authorities of that great country to promote reconstruction, stability and progress in a climate of democracy and respect for the rule of law.

Throughout the region, the international community is continuing to work for reconciliation, the rehabilitation of combatants and reconstruction. It is now more necessary than ever to renounce violence as a political tool and promote dialogue. Refugees and internally displaced persons must be allowed to return to their homes in conditions of dignity, security and justice. They must be rapidly reintegrated into society, together with combatants, whose rehabilitation is essential if they are not to become the cause of new tensions.

I have recently taken measures to strengthen the International Tribunal for Rwanda and ensure that those responsible for the genocide and other crimes committed during the tragic conflict in that country in 1994 are brought to justice.

We must put an end to impunity so that yesterday's injustices do not become tomorrow's problems. The many peace efforts now under way cannot succeed without the unfailing political will of the Central African States themselves.

This inescapable fact was recognized by the Heads of State and Government at their recent summit in Yaoundé in July. The Final Declaration which they adopted on that occasion recognizes the central role which the States of the subregion themselves must play in ensuring their own security.

It was this same conviction that led to the joint decision of Central and West African States to set up an intra-African force to restore peace in the Central African Republic.

You also recognized in Yaoundé that lasting peace can be built only in a climate of socio-economic progress, democratization and the rule of law. I must emphasize the importance of these factors which, under the general heading of "good governance", place the dignity and welfare of the individual at the centre of public policy and government activity. For it is in terms of the improvement of life for the individual that our efforts must be measured. That is the very essence of the Charter of the United Nations, whose principles and purposes are aimed at building a better world.

This is why it is essential to respect human rights, guarantee equal opportunity and promote a political environment which takes account of each and every one of us. Then, and only then, will we achieve a climate of peace and prosperity for the countries of Central Africa and the continent as a whole.

It was here in Libreville in 1993 that your Committee adopted a Non-Aggression Pact among Central African States. You also decided to set up an early-warning mechanism in Central Africa to prevent disputes within and between States. You also took the remarkable step of organizing the joint training of your military forces to prepare them for future peacekeeping operations.

These measures, if respected, will open the way for a future of lasting peace and cooperation in Central Africa. I therefore call on all States which have not yet done so to sign the Non-Aggression Pact as soon as possible. I also call on all the States concerned to faithfully respect the provisions of the Pact so as to end once and for all the conflicts which are tearing Central Africa apart.

In this connection, I deeply regret the build-up of stocks of weapons in the Central African subregion. While military spending has fallen significantly in all continents, this trend is not necessarily reflected in a uniform reduction or apply to all types of weapons.

I personally am deeply concerned at the growing and often illicit arms traffic in the subregion, especially of small arms.

These weapons are often in civilian hands, thus contributing to a rise in crime and banditry, with their all too familiar destabilizing effects. I therefore strongly urge the Committee to look into restricting the circulation of weapons within the subregion, to limit the build-up of military arsenals and reduce spending on weapons.

Success in this sphere, including the introduction of concrete arms control measures, could have a major impact, not only in reducing the threat of conflict, but also in consolidating peace and promoting the socio-economic development of the countries concerned by reallocating appropriations for arms to constructive uses. You may be sure that I fully support your efforts.

As you are aware, security is a concept which embraces more than just military factors. If we can harness Africa's potential for development purposes, we shall be in a better position to stabilize our societies over the long term.

The international community stands ready to help you in this crucial undertaking and I strongly encourage it to contribute generously to the United Nations Trust Fund set up to assist the Committee.

Let me end, however, by emphasizing once again that peace and security, in Central Africa or anywhere, cannot be imposed from outside. The primary responsibility rests with the leaders of the countries concerned.

The United Nations General Assembly was not mistaken in seeing your Committee as an essential instrument for the building of peace and trust among your States.

On behalf of the United Nations, let me assure you sincerely once again of our full support and cooperation. I wish you every success in your deliberations.

Other Documents

Brazzaville Declaration on Cooperation for Peace and Security in Central Africa
Brazzaville, Congo, 1 September 1995

1. The seventh ministerial meeting of the Standing Advisory Committee on Security Questions in Central Africa was held from 31 August to 1 September 1995 at Brazzaville, and examined the problems of peace and security in the subregion of Central Africa.

2. The Ministers expressed their deep concern at the persistence of tensions and violence in the subregion of Central Africa. They noted that this dangerous situation has led to tremendous losses in human lives, considerable material damage and unspeakable suffering among the population, including the massive movement of refugees. They stressed the fact that the resulting insecurity undermines the development efforts of the Governments and peoples of the subregion despite their considerable natural resources.

3. The Ministers agreed that the proliferation of arms even among the civilian populations, including armed gangs, was the main factor in the violence and insecurity prevailing in the countries of the subregion. They also agreed that socio-political problems, economic difficulties and the problems of refugees and displaced persons were exacerbating tensions within and among States.

4. The Ministers recognized that the primary responsibility for the maintenance of peace and security in the subregion devolved on the Governments and peoples of the countries concerned. They encouraged the efforts being made in this direction by the countries concerned. While welcoming the contribution of other States of the subregion to the process of national reconciliation and re-establishment of peace in these countries, they underlined the importance of the support of the international community as a whole.

5. They once again condemned the acts of genocide and atrocious massacres committed in Rwanda from April to mid-July 1994, the acts of extreme violence in Burundi and all other violation of international humanitarian law and reaffirmed their Governments' commitment and determination to spare no effort to prevent other manifestations of violence.

6. The Ministers reaffirmed their renewed support to the United Nations and expressed their profound gratitude for its tireless efforts at peace-building, peace-keeping and peacemaking and for its emergency humanitarian assistance to the subregion, in Africa and throughout the world. They conveyed their congratulations to the States members of the Committee that participated in United Nations peace-keeping operations, in particular, Cameroon, Congo, Chad and Zaire. They especially welcomed and expressed their support for the deployment of the United Nations Angola Verification Mission (UNAVEM III) and the initiation of operations to consolidate the historic peace agreements between the Government of Angola and the National Union for the Total Independence of Angola (UNITA), which were mediated by the United Nations. They also expressed their support for the current United Nations peace efforts in Burundi and Rwanda.

7. The Ministers also agreed that lasting solutions to the manifold challenges facing Angola, Burundi and Rwanda and the Central African subregion in general could

be found only in the framework of close cooperation among the international community, the Organization of African Unity (OAU) and the subregional institutions both directly and indirectly concerned. They particularly welcomed the recent visit of United Nations Secretary-General Boutros Boutros-Ghali to Angola, Burundi, Rwanda and Zaire, which helped further to open up prospects for a lasting solution to the conflicts in the subregion.

8. The Ministers launched an appeal for urgent, effective actions aimed at finding lasting, concrete solutions to the disturbing problem of refugees and displaced persons in the subregion. They expressed their deep appreciation for the humanitarian assistance provided to the refugees and displaced persons by the United Nations and non-governmental organizations and host countries. They also noted the heavy burden on the host countries, especially in the socio-economic, ecological and security areas. Referring to General Assembly resolution 49/24 of 2 December 1994, they reiterated their support for Zaire's request for special assistance from the international community, to deal with the problems caused by the flow of refugees into its territory. The Ministers considered that the problem of refugees, with Africa being in first place as the region with the largest number of refugees, is a humanitarian challenge and called on the United Nations, the countries of origin and the host countries to work together to ensure that refugees are not used for political purposes or to destabilize the States of the subregion, and to seek ways and means to repatriate them to their countries of origin. To that end the Ministers gave a mandate to the officers of the Committee to carry out missions of solidarity to the countries concerned as soon as possible in order to contribute to the process of re-establishing and strengthening peace in the subregion.

9. The Ministers stressed the fact that the 'me objective of the countries of the

subregion is to improve the standard of living of their peoples. They recognized that this will be possible only in a climate of peace and stability both within and among States. To this end, they underlined that a close relationship exists between security and sustainable development. In view of the considerable support from the United Nations and the international community for the efforts to promote security and development in the subregion, and the urgent need for the subregion to meet the challenges facing them in these two fields, the Ministers decided to hold one of their forthcoming meetings at United Nations Headquarters in order to allow for a broader exchange of views with the organs of the United Nations system.

10. The Ministers entrusted the officers of the Committee with the mission of organizing a subregional conference on the topic "Democratic institutions and peace in Central Africa".

11. Lastly, the Ministers noted that their meeting was taking place at a time when the United Nations was celebrating its fiftieth anniversary and reaffirmed their countries' commitment to the purposes and principles enshrined in the Charter.

A/51/274-S/1996/631, annex

Final Declaration of the First Summit of Heads of State and Government of Countries Members of the United Nations Standing Advisory Committee on Security Questions in Central Africa
Yaoundé, Cameroon, 8 July 1996

1. Due to the persistence and worsening of acts of violence in Central Africa, the First Summit of Heads of State and Government of Countries Members of the United Nations

Standing Advisory Committee on Security Questions in Central Africa was held on 8 July 1996, in Yaoundé, to consider the problems relating to peace and security in the subregion, in accordance with the recommendation of the ministerial meeting of the said Committee.

2. The Heads of State and Government express their deep concern at the continued tensions, crises and conflicts and at the continued violence in Central Africa, which has created a veritable humanitarian tragedy, particularly with regard to the problems of refugees and displaced persons.

3. The Heads of State and Government stress the urgent necessity for States in the subregion to establish, encourage and sustain participatory systems of governance as a means of preventing conflicts. Furthermore, they underscore the necessity to organize, under United Nations auspices, training seminars for officers in the armed forces, republican guard, gendarmerie and police forces of the Central African States, in order to promote a culture of peace by explaining, once again, the role of these forces in a democratic context.

4. The Heads of State and Government agree to take the necessary steps to promote confidence and security between States in the Central Africa subregion. To that end, they are proceeding to sign the Non-Aggression Pact between the States of Central Africa and will see to it that appropriate arrangements are made for its effective implementation.

5. The Heads of State and Government also underscore the necessity for States in the subregion to make greater use of bilateral and subregional consultation mechanisms for the peaceful settlement of their disputes; this would, inter alia, make it possible to settle the thorny problem of refugees and displaced persons in the subregion swiftly and in a satisfactory manner.

6. The Heads of State and Government express their concern at the increased proliferation of weapons, a source of insecurity and a threat to the stability of States in the subregion. In order to contain this scourge they declare that they are in favour of cooperation to fight this phenomenon, inter alia, by establishing a disarmament programme with the assistance of the United Nations and the international community. To that end, they ask their defence and interior ministers to meet as a matter of urgency in order to propose practical modalities for setting up this programme.

7. The Heads of State and Government agree to set up, under United Nations auspices, an early warning system as the basic instrument for preventive diplomacy in Central Africa. They give their foreign affairs, defence and interior ministers a mandate to study, with the United Nations, modalities for establishing such a mechanism.

8. The Heads of State and Government reaffirm their decision to create model peace-keeping units within the armed forces, gendarmerie, republican guard and police forces of States members, which will be made available to the United Nations and the Organization of African Unity in the context of peace-keeping operations. They note with satisfaction the specific measures taken to that end by States members. They also welcome the arrangements made by the United Nations with a view to ensuring the establishment of the said units.

9. The Heads of State and Government underscore the necessity to strengthen cooperation between States in the subregion and bilateral and multilateral partners concerning peace and security in Central Africa. Accordingly, they express their gratitude to those partners who have contributed and who will contribute to the

United Nations trust fund for the implementation of the Committee's programme.

10.   The Heads of State and Government welcome the establishment by the United Nations General Assembly, in 1992, of the United Nations Standing Advisory Committee on Security Questions in Central Africa. They express their gratitude to the United Nations for the support it continues to provide to the Committee. They decide to meet periodically to consider issues relating to peace and security in Central Africa.

===

Non-Aggression Pact among the Member States of the United Nations Standing Advisory Committee on Security Questions in Central Africa
Signed at Yaoundé, Cameroon, on 8 July 1996

THE HIGH CONTRACTING PARTIES,

Bearing in mind that the harmonious relations which exist among the peoples and States members of the United Nations Standing Advisory Committee on Security Questions in Central Africa can be maintained and strengthened only in a climate of peace and security that is favourable to economic and social development,

Considering Article 2, paragraph 4, of the United Nations Charter, which requires that all Members refrain in their international relations from the threat or use of force, either against the territorial integrity or independence of any State, or in any other manner inconsistent with the purposes of the United Nations,

Considering declaration AHG/DECL.3 (XXIX), adopted at the twenty-ninth ordinary session of the Heads of State and

Government of the Organization of African Unity (OAU) in June 1993, establishing, within the OAU, a mechanism for conflict prevention, management and resolution,

Considering the decision taken by the Secretary-General of the United Nations on 28 May 1992 to establish the Standing Advisory Committee on Security Questions in Central Africa, pursuant to United Nations General Assembly resolution 46/37 B,

Bearing in mind the conclusions of the organizational meeting of the United Nations Standing Advisory Committee on Security Questions in Central Africa, held at Yaoundé in July 1992, and endorsed by United Nations General Assembly resolution 47/53 F of 15 December 1992,

Reaffirming their commitment to promoting a policy of cooperation and pursuing the objectives of peace, security, disarmament and development in the subregion,

HAVE AGREED AS FOLLOWS:

Article I
Member States undertake to refrain in their mutual relations from the threat or use of force or aggression, either against the territorial integrity or independence of other member States, or in any other manner inconsistent with the Charter of the United Nations, the Charter of the Organization of African Unity or the treaty establishing the Economic Community of Central African States (ECCAS).

Article II
Each member State undertakes to refrain from committing, encouraging or supporting acts of hostility or aggression against the territorial integrity or independence of other member States.

Article III
Each member State undertakes to ensure that the acts referred to in Article 2

above are not committed from its territory by resident or nonresident aliens against the sovereignty or territorial integrity of other member States.

Article IV

Member States undertake to resort to peaceful means to settle any differences that may arise among them by having recourse to the various relevant mechanisms for resolving conflicts within the Economic Community of Central African States, the Organization of African Unity and/or the United Nations.

Article V

The present Pact may be supplemented by additional protocols.

Article VI

1. The present Pact, shall enter into force as soon as it has bean ratified by at least seven of the signatory States, following the constitutional procedures of each member State;

2. The present Pact, the English and French texts of which are equally authentic, and all instruments of ratification thereof, shall be deposited with the Government of the country which hosts the signing of said Pact, depositary, which shall transmit certified copies of the Pact to all member States, notify them of the dates on which the instruments of ratification are deposited and register the present text with the United Nations and the Organization of African Unity.

IN WITNESS WHEREOF the undersigned, duly authorized, have signed this Pact.

Done at __Yaoundé__ on __08 July 1996__

FOR:

ANGOLA	_____
BURUNDI	*signed*
CAMEROON	*signed*
CENTRAL AFRICAN REPUBLIC	*signed (24/09/96)*
CHAD	*signed*
CONGO	*signed*
EQUATORIAL GUINEA	*signed*
GABON	*signed*
RWANDA	
SAO TOME AND PRINCIPE	*signed*
ZAIRE	*signed*

S/1996/1006, annex

Declaration of the Second Summit Meeting of Heads of State and Government of the Countries Members of the United Nations Standing Advisory Committee on Security Questions in Central Africa

Brazzaville, Congo, 2-3 December 1996

We, the heads of State and Government of the countries members of the United Nations Standing Advisory Committee on Security Questions in Central Africa:

The Republic of Angola
The Republic of Burundi
The Republic of Cameroon
The Central African Republic
The Republic of Chad
The Republic of the Congo
The Republic of Equatorial Guinea
The Gabonese Republic
The Democratic Republic of Sao Tome and Principe
The Republic of Zaire

met in Brazzaville on 2 and 3 December 1996, and, having reviewed the serious problems concerned with peace and security in Central Africa, particularly the situation in the Great Lakes region,

I. GENERAL CONTEXT

1. Note with profound concern that the situation in the subregion as a whole not only continues to be very worrying, but has deteriorated in certain parts of the subregion

since the last summit meeting of the Committee, held on 8 July 1996 in Yaoundé.

2. Express serious concern at the latest developments in the Great Lakes region, particularly in eastern Zaire and the Central African Republic.

3. Welcome the progress towards peace and national reconciliation in Angola and strongly encourage our Angolan brothers to resolve the military questions and embark as quickly as possible on the political phase, in accordance with the Lusaka Protocol and Security Council resolution 1075 (1996) of 11 October 1996, in order to consolidate the peace process and allow the Angolan people to direct their efforts towards the task of national reconstruction.

4. Strongly condemn the threat or use of force as a means of resolving problems either within or between States.

5. Deeply deplore the loss of so many human lives, the material damage and the indescribable suffering caused by armed conflicts in the subregion, which are generating millions of refugees and displaced persons, and express our deep gratitude to the countries and peoples of the subregion for their generous and fraternal hospitality and welcome.

6. Recognize that our countries and our peoples are united by natural and historical bonds of fraternity and solidarity, and commit ourselves to the task of consolidating those bonds.

7. Welcome the recent signing by Burundi, Cameroon, the Central African Republic, Chad, the Congo, Equatorial Guinea, Gabon, Sao Tome and Principe and Zaire of the Non-Aggression Pact between Central African States, and invite all States members of the Committee that have not yet done so to sign it as soon as possible, insofar as the Pact is one of the most important measures of trust among the States in the subregion.

8. Reaffirm our pledge to use bilateral and multilateral consultative machinery for the settlement of inter-State disputes and to give priority to dialogue and consensus-seeking for the resolution of internal conflicts, in accordance with the common African tradition.

9. Also reaffirm our pledge to respect the fundamental principles embodied in the Charter of the United Nations and the Charter of the Organization of African Unity (OAU), particularly:

(a) The sovereign equality of all States;

(b) Non-interference in the internal affairs of States;

(c) Respect for the sovereignty and territorial integrity of every State;

(d) The peaceful settlement of disputes;

(e) The inviolability of internationally recognized borders.

10. Recognize the inalienable right of States to reaffirm the central authority of the State wherever it is threatened within internationally recognized borders.

11. Reaffirm the joint decision taken by member States to take a more active part in United Nations and OAU peace operations, particularly in the subregion.

Also reaffirm, in this connection, the decision to set up specialized peacekeeping units within our armed forces.

Request our bilateral and multilateral partners, with the support of the United Nations, to respond to the urgent requests for logistical equipment and training for the above-mentioned units.

12. Reiterate the urgent need for

member States to set up, promote and support participatory systems of government and to promote human rights and the rule of law as means of preventing conflicts and ensuring the stability of States, and stress, in this respect, the need to organize workshops for the security forces of member States in order to promote a culture of peace by redefining their role in a democratic context.

II. THE SITUATION IN THE GREAT LAKES REGION

13. Stress the need for an integrated and comprehensive approach to the search for a lasting peace in the Great Lakes region, taking into account the complexity of the challenges facing this area of the subregion, particularly in the humanitarian, security-related and political fields.

Humanitarian questions

14. Express our dismay at the indecisiveness of the international community when faced with the suffering of our brothers in the Great Lakes region, and commit ourselves unreservedly to the task of intensifying our efforts to put an end to the humanitarian crisis affecting this part of the subregion of Central Africa.

15. Express our gratitude to the United Republic of Tanzania and Zaire for accepting the majority of refugees from the Great Lakes region in their territory, and call for greater international assistance to be given directly to these countries and other countries offering asylum to help them to confront the economic, environmental and any other consequences of the massive influx of refugees in their territory.

16. Stress the need for consultation with the States of the Great Lakes region directly involved in humanitarian operations and also stress the benefits of strengthening cooperation on humanitarian questions amongst the members of the Standing Advisory Committee, by facilitating delivery of humanitarian assistance to the recipients and by involving the specialized units in peace operations.

17. Note the efforts being made by Burundi and Rwanda to receive and reintegrate refugees in conditions of security and dignity, and encourage those countries to continue such efforts.

18. Note the measures already taken by the Government of Burundi to restore the democratic process in that country, and take note of its commitment to expedite the creation of democratic institutions within a reasonable time-frame by giving priority to dialogue with the political class as a whole and all the segments of Burundian society.

19. Invite the States parties to the Arusha Accords to lift the embargo which has a greater effect on the Burundian people, especially the most vulnerable social classes.

Security questions

20. Are convinced that the uncontrolled proliferation of weapons and recourse to the use of force to settle differences are major contributing factors to the instability and tensions which dominate the Great Lakes region.

Encourage therefore all parties in Burundi to choose a form of mediation which guarantees objectivity and neutrality in order to move ahead in the peace process, in the interests of the people of Burundi.

The officers of the Standing Advisory Committee on Security Questions in Central Africa will support such measures.

21. Strongly condemn any actions or measures which violate the territorial integrity of any State of the Great Lakes region, pursuant to resolution 16 of the first

OAU summit meeting held in Cairo in 1964.

22. Stress the need for each State to create a truly republican army in order to guarantee stability, security and confidence within its territory, and call upon the bilateral and multilateral partners to support the stricken countries' efforts to restore the authority of the State.

Political questions

23. Maintain that true peace and security in this part of our subregion are based on establishing and consolidating democracy and participatory systems of government which take into account the specific nature of each State. With that in mind, we call on the countries members of the Committee to act as mediators between the parties involved, when asked to do so.

24. Consider that impunity is a threat to the peace and stability of States, and in that context invite all States to cooperate with the International Tribunal for Rwanda in accordance with United Nations Security Council resolution 955 (1994).

III. FOLLOW-UP MEASURES

25. Decide to give priority to monitoring the situation in the Great Lakes region and to consult regularly on developments with a view to finding peaceful solutions.

26. Request the officers of the Committee to take practical steps to establish the subregional early warning mechanism as a basic tool of preventive diplomacy in Central Africa and to submit a report to the heads of State and Government of the member countries by the end of June 1997.

27. Ask the ministers of defence and of the interior of the member States to hold an emergency joint meeting with a view to proposing practical measures for subregional cooperation in combating the uncontrolled proliferation of weapons and illegal drug trafficking, and also request the officers of the Committee to submit a report to the heads of State and Government.

28. Decide to convene a ministerial level subregional conference in February 1997 in Brazzaville on the question of "Democratic institutions and peace in Central Africa", and stress the importance of participation by all the States of the subregion at that conference.

29. Request the officers to contact the bilateral and multilateral partners to solicit their contributions to the Trust Fund established by the United Nations, for the purpose of giving a new impetus to the Committee's activities and to the implementation, as a priority, of the measures contained in this declaration.

30. Profoundly regret that at the dawn of the twenty-first century, when the world has so many opportunities for scientific and technological progress, full participation in that process by Africa in general and by the subregion in particular remains hampered by the growing number of conflicts and by political instability. In that context we reaffirm the primary responsibility incumbent upon every State to guarantee the security and well-being of its peoples, and stress the need to promote development through science as a means of preventing conflicts and ensuring the political stability of States.

31. Support the Central African Republic in its efforts, through the measures which it is taking within the framework of established democratic institutions, to restore peace, harmony and stability in that country.

32. Lastly, express our satisfaction with the climate of cordiality, understanding and fraternity which prevailed during the summit meeting.

A/52/283* - S/1997/644*

Report of the Ninth Ministerial Meeting of the United Nations Standing Advisory Committee on Security Questions in Central Africa

Libreville, Gabon, 7-11 July 1997

INTRODUCTION

1.   The ninth meeting of the United Nations Standing Advisory Committee on Security Questions in Central Africa was held at Libreville from 7 to 11 July 1997 at the ministerial level.

2.   The following States members took part in the meeting: Angola, Burundi, Cameroon, Chad, Central African Republic, Congo, Democratic Republic of the Congo, Equatorial Guinea, Gabon and Sao Tome and Principe.

3.   Rwanda was unable to attend.

4.   The following participated in the work of the meeting as observers: the representative of the Secretary-General of the United Nations; the representative of the Secretary-General of the Organization of African Unity (OAU); the representative of the United Nations Development Programme (UNDP); and the representative of the Agency for Cultural and Technical Cooperation.

5.   At the invitation of the Government of Gabon, the five permanent members of the United Nations Security Council were invited to the meeting. Representatives of China, France, the Russian Federation and the United States of America attended the meeting. The United Kingdom was unable to attend.

6.   At the opening ceremony of the meeting statements were made by: the current President of the Committee, His Excellency Mr. Destin Arsène Tsaty-Boungou, Minister for Foreign Affairs and Cooperation and Francophone Affairs of the Republic of the Congo; Mr. Mohamed Sahnoun, the representative of the Secretaries General of the United Nations and of the Organization of African Unity for the Great Lakes region, who read out a message from the Secretary-General of the United Nations; and H.E. Dr. Paulin Obame Nguema, Prime Minister, Head of Government of the Gabonese Republic, who formally opened the meeting.

A. Adoption of the agenda

7. The Committee adopted the following agenda:

    1.   Election of officers.
    2.   Review of the activities of the Committee.
    3.   Review of the geopolitical situation in Central Africa.
    4.   Involvement of the officers of the Committee in the peace processes in Central Africa and review of the plan of action of the Committee.
    5.   Exchange of views on improving cooperation for conflict prevention and management in Central Africa: the role of the permanent members of the Security Council.
    6.   Recommendations.
    7.   Consideration and adoption of the final report of the ninth meeting of the Committee.

B. Progress of work

1. Election of officers

8. The Committee elected new officers as follows: Chairman: Gabon; First Vice-Chairman: Angola; Second Vice-President: Chad; Rapporteur: Burundi.

2. Review of the activities of the Committee

9. The Committee took note of the report submitted by His Excellency Mr. Destin Arsène Tsaty-Boungou, Minister for Foreign Affairs and Cooperation and Francophonie Affairs of the Republic of the Congo, in his capacity as outgoing Chairman.

10. The report reflected increased recognition of the role played by the Committee in the search for ways and means to find solutions to the ongoing crises and conflicts in the subregion.

11. The Committee also noted the effective involvement of the heads of State and Government of member countries in its activities, in particular their participation in 1996 in the Yaoundé and Brazzaville summit meetings.

12. The Committee recalled that at the Yaoundé summit meeting, which was held alongside the thirty-second summit meeting of OAU, eight heads of State and Government had solemnly signed the Non-Aggression Pact. To date, nine States members of the Committee have signed the Pact.

13. The Committee noted that Angola had reaffirmed its willingness to sign the Pact as soon as possible. It appealed to Rwanda to do likewise and invited member States which had already signed the Pact to ratify it with a view to its entry into force.

14. The outgoing Chairman also stressed the Committee's contribution to the search for solutions to the crisis in the former Zaire, and welcomed the organization of a training seminar for instructors in peacekeeping operations.

15. The outgoing officers made preparations for the subregional conference on the topic "Democratic institutions and peace in Central Africa", which was to be held before the end of 1997.

16. Lastly, the officers took note of the study prepared at their request by the Committee secretariat on the establishment of a subregional early warning mechanism, to be based in Libreville, Gabon. The project had been submitted to UNDP with a request for assistance in financing that mechanism.

17. The Committee commended the outgoing Chairman for the efforts he had made in the exercise of his mandate.

3. Review of the geopolitical situation in Central Africa

18. Introducing the item, the new Chairman, His Excellency Mr. Casimir Oye Mba, Minister of State and Minister for Foreign Affairs and Cooperation of the Gabonese Republic, noted with concern the deterioration of the situation of peace and stability in many of the Committee's member countries. He stressed the indivisible nature of subregional peace and security, emphasizing that no country in Central Africa would experience lasting peace as long as areas of tension remained in other countries of the subregion.

Democratic Republic of the Congo

19. The Committee welcomed the calming of the situation after the upheaval which had taken place in the Democratic Republic of the Congo and noted with satisfaction the determination of the United Nations to work closely with the new authorities of that country with a view to ensuring its reconstruction, stability and progress in respect for democratic principles and the rule of law.

Burundi

20. The Committee welcomed the improvement in the overall situation in Burundi and encouraged the Government of Burundi to continue the dialogue with all the parties to the conflict with a view to restoring

the democratic process and establishing all the necessary conditions for true national reconciliation.

21. Concerned about the dire consequences of the embargo against Burundi for the most vulnerable social groups in that country, the Committee once again issued an appeal to the States parties to the Arusha Accords for the total lifting of the embargo.

22. Noting the great efforts made by States to receive refugees in their territories, the Committee stressed the need for host countries to ensure that the international conventions relating to the status of refugees were fully respected. The Committee also urged the countries of origin to establish conditions to facilitate the return of the refugees to their respective countries in dignity and security.

Republic of the Congo

23. The Committee expressed deep concern about the political and military crisis which was engulfing the Republic of the Congo and was causing much loss of innocent human life.

24. It urged the parties to the conflict to do everything possible to bring about an end to the hostilities by promoting legal and political solutions based on constitutional provisions.

25. The Committee also made an appeal to the international community and to the United Nations Security Council in particular for the rapid deployment of a United Nations peacekeeping force in the Congo to help promote the democratic process in that country.

Angola

26. The Committee welcomed the positive developments in the situation in Angola which had been marked by the installation,

on 11 April 1997, of a Government of national unity, which included representatives of the União Nacional para a Independencia Total de Angola (UNITA), and by the return to the National Assembly of UNITA deputies.

27. The Committee expressed support for that process, which paved the way for the full implementation of the Lusaka Protocol, and called on all the parties to work in good faith for the establishment of lasting peace with a view to national reconciliation. In that respect, it supported the efforts of the Angolan Government to prevent any action which might endanger the full implementation of the Lusaka Protocol.

Chad

28. The Committee noted with satisfaction the restoration of peace in Chad and the consolidation of the democratic process in that country.

29. It welcomed the efforts made by the Government of Chad to combat illicit arms trafficking.

30. The Committee also commended the efforts which had led to a reduction in the size of the army and strongly appealed to the international community to support the Government of Chad in the reintegration of demobilized soldiers in society.

Cameroon

31. With regard to Cameroon, the Committee expressed its concern about the persistence of tension and military incidents in the disputed area of Bakassi. It called on the International Court of Justice to speed up the case in progress with a view to bringing about a final settlement of the dispute.

32. The Committee also noted the success of the recent elections in Cameroon.

Sao Tome and Principe

33. The Committee noted with satisfaction the significant efforts made by the Government of Sao Tome and Principe in 1997 to consolidate the democratic process in that country.

Central African Republic

34. In the Central African Republic, the Committee welcomed the improvement of the political and security situation and commended the decisive role played at the local level by the international monitoring committee in facilitating the work of the Inter-African Force to Monitor the Implementation of the Bangui Agreements (MISAB). The Committee welcomed the efforts of General Amadou Toumani Touré, which had led to the signing of a ceasefire agreement on 2 July 1997 and the adoption of a timetable for the reintegration of mutinous soldiers and their weapons in their respective barracks.

35. The Committee believed that the return of the soldiers to their respective units constituted significant progress which should mark the end of the uprising in that country.

Equatorial Guinea

36. The Committee welcomed the efforts made in Equatorial Guinea to consolidate the democratic process in that country. In that connection it took note of the signing of a national pact between the Government and all the political parties and of a document to evaluate that pact.

4. Involvement of the officers of the Committee in the peace processes in Central Africa and consideration of the plan of action of the Committee

37. The current disturbing situation in the subregion and the need to take effective steps for crisis and conflict prevention would, according to the Committee's previous recommendations, require greater involvement of the officers of the Committee in current and future mediation efforts.

38. The Committee therefore called upon its Chairman to use his good offices and to participate fully in the mediation of the crisis and conflict situations in the subregion.

39. The Committee agreed that its activities should be based on the following programme of action.

Political and diplomatic measures

40. Considering the seriousness of the situation in the Republic of the Congo and the imperative need to end the violence plaguing that country, the Committee fully supports the appeal made to the Security Council by His Excellency El Hadj Omar Bongo, President of the Gabonese Republic and head of the International Mediation Committee, for the deployment of an intervention force in that country. In this connection, the Committee strongly encourages member States to participate in such a force.

41. The Committee mandates its President and the other officers of the Committee to meet with the Secretary-General of the United Nations during the fifty-second session of the General Assembly to request his ongoing support for the Committee's efforts. On that occasion, the officers will convey the Committee's desire to revert to its initial practice of holding two ministerial meetings a year.

42. The Committee mandates its officers, during their stay in New York, to pursue consultations with the members of the Security Council with a view to strengthening cooperation between that body and the countries of Central Africa in seeking ways and means of consolidating peace in the subregion.

43. The Committee mandates its officers to contact the United Nations Secretariat, the United Nations Development Programme (UNDP), the European Union and other partners of the subregion to ensure the effective establishment of the early warning mechanism, preferably by the end of 1997.

44. As proposed by the outgoing Chairman, the Committee recommends that a conference be held by the end of the year on the topic "Democratic institutions and peace in Central Africa". The Committee welcomes the offer of Equatorial Guinea to host this conference. The Committee requests its Chairman to contact the Government of Equatorial Guinea to confirm the date, place and organizational arrangements for this important conference.

45. Considering the importance of the Non-Aggression Pact, the Committee mandates the Chairman to approach the Angolan and Rwandan authorities with a view to obtaining their signatures.

46. The Committee takes note of the message from the Secretary-General of the Organization of African Unity (OAU) to the ninth ministerial meeting. It welcomes that Organization's willingness to make concerted efforts towards peace, in cooperation with subregional institutions, and requests its Chairman to contact the OAU General Secretariat with a view to establishing specific modalities of cooperation between that body and the Committee.

47. The Committee requests the OAU to provide assistance, within the limits of its resources, for the implementation of the Committee's plan of action.

Defence and security measures

48. As requested by the heads of State and Government of the countries members of the Committee, the Committee once again calls upon the ministers of defence and of the interior of its member countries to meet no later than December 1997 to draw up a practical programme for combating the illegal circulation of weapons and drugs in the subregion. Member States are invited to submit their suggestions to the Chairman by the end of September 1997 so that he may prepare a draft programme for consideration at the meeting.

49. The Committee mandates its Chairman to request the assistance and cooperation of the United Nations Secretariat, UNDP, the World Bank, the European Union and other organizations in helping the relevant countries of the subregion to set up programmes for demobilizing militias and former combatants, discharging them from military service and reintegrating them into civilian life.

50. Based on the experience acquired in the training seminar on peacekeeping operations organized by the Committee in Yaoundé in September 1996, the Committee calls upon the ministers of defence to identify ways of building the subregion's peacekeeping capacity. In this connection, the Committee mandates its Chairman to seek the support of the United Nations Secretariat for the organization of additional seminars to train subregional personnel in peacekeeping operations.

51. Accordingly, the Committee reiterates the importance of expediting the establishment of peacekeeping units within the armed forces of member countries.

52. As a practical means of ensuring that the countries of the subregion are better prepared to participate effectively in future peacekeeping operations, the Committee underscores the importance of organizing joint military exercises to simulate the conduct of standard peacekeeping operations. To this end, the Committee calls upon its Chairman to submit proposals by the end of October 1997 on arrange-ments for holding such exercises in March 1998.

53. The Committee mandates its Chairman to seek assistance from the United Nations Secretariat, the United Nations Educational, Scientific and Cultural Organization (UNESCO), the European Union, the Agency for Cultural and Technical Co-operation and the rest of the international community for the organization of seminars to familiarize the armed forces and security forces with respect for the rule of law and the army's role in a democracy.

54. Considering that the organization of sporting events between the armies of the States of the subregion is likely to enhance brotherhood in arms and to promote mutual confidence between States, the Committee requests the Supreme Council for Sport in Africa (SCSA) and the Organization for Military Sport in Africa to study the possibility of giving a new impetus to the organization of military sports competitions in Central Africa.

5. Exchange of views on improving cooperation for conflict prevention and management in Central Africa: The role of the permanent members of the Security Council

55. At the invitation of the Gabonese Government, the representatives of China, France, the United States of America and the Russian Federation took part in the work of the Committee. The United Kingdom was unable to do so.

56. During the exchange of views, the permanent members unanimously recognized the importance of the Committee's work and confirmed the commitment made in Denver, during the G-8 summit, to help African countries, and particularly those in Central Africa, to build their capacities in the area of peacekeeping and conflict prevention. They recognized the crucial importance of setting up structures and initiatives designed to prevent the outbreak of armed conflicts.

57. In that context, the representative of France reported to the Committee on the joint initiative which his country, the United States of America and the United Kingdom were carrying out with a view to building African peacekeeping capacity.

58. The representative of the United States of America, in turn, reported to the Committee on the programmes which his country was implementing, both alone and with its partners, to help build African capacities for prevention, conflict settlement and peacekeeping activities. He listed a number of preconditions for the deployment of a peacekeeping operation by the Security Council. He emphasized, inter alia, that an effective ceasefire must be observed before a decision could be taken to deploy a peacekeeping operation.

59. The representative of China, while regretting the persistence of conflicts in Africa which resulted in the loss of human lives and significant material damage, reaffirmed his country's support for the efforts being made by the Central African countries to settle their differences peacefully. He said that his country would examine carefully the plan of action adopted by the Committee at the current meeting.

60. The representative of the Russian Federation highlighted the need to promote peacekeeping activities and to establish a more reliable system of crisis detection and prevention.

61. The representative of UNDP said that his organization supported the initiative to establish an early warning mechanism in Central Africa. In that connection, he informed the Committee that the Regional Bureau for Africa and the Emergency Response Division at UNDP headquarters were studying the plan for financing the mechanism which the Committee secretariat had submitted to them at the request of the officers.

62. The Committee, while recognizing that its members had the primary responsibility for peacekeeping in their countries, requested the assistance of the members of the Security Council in implementing its plan of action for peace and stability in Central Africa.

RECOMMENDATIONS

63. The Committee, having underscored the crucial role played by the Inter-African Force to Monitor the Implementation of the Bangui Agreements (MISAB) in resolving the Central African crisis, requests its Chairman to bring the matter before the General Assembly, the Security Council and the Secretary-General of the United Nations in order to seek their assistance to MISAB so that it could implement the Bangui peace agreements fully.

64. To strengthen the Committee's activities and to enable it to respond more effectively to the subregion's need for conflict prevention and conflict settlement initiatives in Central Africa, the Committee requests its Chairman to convey to the Secretary-General of the United Nations its strong desire to revive its practice of holding two annual meetings at the ministerial level.

65. While thanking the countries which have contributed to the United Nations Trust Fund set up by the Secretary-General to finance the implementation of the Committee's programme of activities, the Committee again appeals to all States and to the international community to continue to give generously to the Fund.

Security Council Resolution establishing the International Criminal Tribunal for Rwanda

The Security Council,

Reaffirming all its previous resolutions on the situation in Rwanda,

Having considered the reports of the Secretary-General pursuant to paragraph 3 of resolution 935 (1994) of 1 July 1994 (S/1994/879 and S/1994/906), and having taken note of the reports of the Special Rapporteur for Rwanda of the United Nations Commission on Human Rights (S/1994/1157, annex I and annex II),

Expressing appreciation for the work of the Commission of Experts established pursuant to resolution 935 (1994), in particular its preliminary report on violations of international humanitarian law in Rwanda transmitted by the Secretary-General's letter of 1 October 1994 (S/1994/1125),

Expressing once again its grave concern at the reports indicating that genocide and other systematic, widespread and flagrant violations of international humanitarian law have been committed in Rwanda,

Determining that this situation continues to constitute a threat to international peace and security,

Determined to put an end to such crimes and to take effective measures to bring to justice the persons who are responsible for them,

Convinced that in the particular circumstances of Rwanda, the prosecution of persons responsible for serious violations of international humanitarian law would enable this aim to be achieved and would contribute to the process of national reconciliation and to the restoration and maintenance of peace,

Believing that the establishment of an international tribunal for the prosecution of persons responsible for genocide and the other above-mentioned violations of international humanitarian law will contribute to ensuring that such violations are halted and effectively redressed,

Stressing also the need for international cooperation to strengthen the courts and judicial system of Rwanda, having regard in particular to the necessity for those courts to deal with large numbers of suspects,

Considering that the Commission of Experts established pursuant to resolution 935 (1994) should continue on an urgent basis the collection of information relating to evidence of grave violations of international humanitarian law committed in the territory of Rwanda and should submit its final report to the Secretary-General by 30 November 1994,

Acting under Chapter VII of the Charter of the United Nations,

1. Decides hereby, having received the request of the Government of Rwanda (S/1994/1115), to establish an international tribunal for the sole purpose of prosecuting persons responsible for genocide and other serious violations of international humanitarian law committed in the territory of Rwanda and Rwandan citizens responsible for genocide and other such violations committed in the territory of neighbouring States, between 1 January 1994 and 31 December 1994 and to this end to adopt the Statute of the International Criminal Tribunal for Rwanda annexed hereto;

2. Decides that all States shall cooperate fully with the International Tribunal and its organs in accordance with the present resolution and the Statute of the International Tribunal and that consequently all States shall take any measures necessary under their domestic law to implement the provisions of the present resolution and the Statute, including the obligation of States to comply with requests for assistance or orders issued by a Trial Chamber under Article 28 of the Statute, and requests States to keep the Secretary-General informed of such measures;

3. Considers that the Government of Rwanda should be notified prior to the taking of decisions under articles 26 and 27 of the Statute;

4. Urges States and inter-governmental and non-governmental organizations to contribute funds, equipment and services to the International Tribunal, including the offer of expert personnel;

5. Requests the Secretary-General to implement this resolution urgently and in particular to make practical arrangements for the effective functioning of the International Tribunal, including recommendations to the Council as to possible locations for the seat of the International Tribunal at the earliest time and to report periodically to the Council;

6. Decides that the seat of the International Tribunal shall be determined by the Council having regard to considerations of justice and fairness as well as administrative efficiency, including access to witnesses, and economy, and subject to the conclusion of appropriate arrangements between the United Nations and the State of the seat, acceptable to the Council, having regard to the fact that the International Tribunal may meet away from its seat when it considers it necessary for the efficient exercise of its functions; and decides that an office will be established and proceedings will be conducted in Rwanda, where feasible and appropriate, subject to the conclusion of similar appropriate arrangements;

7. <u>Decides</u> to consider increasing the number of judges and Trial Chambers of the International Tribunal if it becomes necessary;

8. <u>Decides</u> to remain actively seized of the matter.

<u>3453rd meeting</u>
<u>8 November 1994</u>

A/50/474, annex II

Typology of Sources of Conflict in the Central African Subregion

(adopted at the sixth ministerial meeting of the UN Standing Advisory Committee, Brazzaville, Congo, March 1995)

Bearing in mind the recent experience of the countries of the Central African subregion, a number of sources of tension, crisis and conflict have been identified, especially at the internal and inter-State levels and outside the subregion.

I. <u>Sources of internal conflict</u>

At the internal level, the main sources of conflict are as follows:

(a) Exacerbation of ethnic, cultural, religious and political differences;

(b) Arms proliferation among population groups, leading to banditry and terrorism;

(c) Early experience with democracy and democratic management, and failure to respect minority rights;

(d) Irresolute desires for secession;

(e) Coups d'état;

(f) Armed opposition movements;

(g) Widening civil wars;

(h) Major disasters;

(I) Poverty;

(j) Social injustice.

II. <u>Sources of inter-state conflict</u>

At the inter-State level, the main sources of conflict are as follows:

(a) Border disputes, especially those relating to the delimitation of borders and to neighbourly relations;

(b) Problems concerning refugees, displaced persons and illegal immigration;

(c) Desire for power.

III. <u>Sources of conflict from outside the subregion</u>

Sources of conflict from outside the subregion include the following:

(a) Aggression of all kinds by third States;

(b) Interference of all kinds by third States;

(c) Deployment of forces;

(d) Desire for power.

United Nations Press Releases
*dealing with the UN Standing Advisory Committee
on Security Questions in Central Africa*

SG/A/496 - 28 May 1992

SECRETARY-GENERAL ANNOUNCES ESTABLISHMENT OF STANDING ADVISORY COMMITTEE ON SECURITY QUESTIONS IN CENTRAL AFRICA

Secretary-General Boutros Boutros-Ghali today announced the establishment of the Standing Advisory Committee on Security Questions in Central Africa, in accordance with General Assembly resolution 46/37 B, entitled "Regional confidence-building measures", adopted by consensus on 6 December 1991. In that resolution, the Assembly welcomed the initiative taken by the States members of the Economic Community of Central African States to create, under the auspices of the United Nations, a standing advisory committee on security questions in Central Africa and requested the Secretary-General to establish such a committee.

The purpose of the Committee will be to develop confidence-building measures and measures to promote arms restraint and development in the subregion of Central Africa. The membership of the Committee will comprise the 10 States members of the Economic Community of the Central African States: Burundi, Cameroon, Central African Republic, Chad, Congo, Equatorial Guinea, Gabon, Rwanda, Sao Tome and Principe and Zaire. It is envisaged that discussions in the Committee will be at different levels, including expert sessions (at the level of senior military and civilian officials), ministerial meetings and discussions by the Heads of State concerned during their annual meetings within the framework of the Economic Community of Central African States.

The Committee will hold its organizational meeting in Yaounde, Cameroon, shortly. The meeting is expected to be held at the ministerial level. Sammy Buo, of the Office for Disarmament Affairs of the Department for Political Affairs, has been designated Secretary of the Standing Advisory Committee.

DC/2444 - 2 August 1993

STANDING ADVISORY COMMITTEE ON SECURITY QUESTIONS IN CENTRAL AFRICA TO MEET IN LIBREVILLE, 30 AUGUST-3 SEPTEMBER

NEW YORK, 2 August (Office for Disarmament Affairs) - - The Standing Advisory Committee on Security Questions in Central Africa will hold the second of its two scheduled meetings for 1993 in Libreville, Gabon, from 30 August to 3 September. The meeting will be at the ministerial level. The Committee last met in Bujumbura, Burundi, from 6 to 12 March, also at the ministerial level.

Secretary-General Boutros Boutros-Ghali on 28 May 1992 announced the establishment of the Committee in accordance with General Assembly resolution 46/37B on regional confidence-building measures, adopted by consensus on 6 December 1991. In that resolution, the Assembly welcomed the initiative taken by the States members of the Economic Community of Central African States to create, under the auspices of the United Nations, a standing advisory committee on security questions in central Africa and requested the Secretary-General to establish such a committee. The Committee held its organizational meeting in Yaounde, Cameroon, from 27 to 31 July

1992, and adopted a programme of work which was subsequently endorsed by the General Assembly.

The purpose of the Committee is to develop confidence-building measures and to promote arms restraint and development in the subregion of central Africa. Discussions in the Committee take place at different levels, including expert sessions at the level of senior military and civilian officials, ministerial meetings and discussions by Heads of State during their annual meetings within the framework of the Economic Community of Central African States.

Issues to be discussed at the forthcoming meeting in Libreville include some priority subjects such as the elaboration of a non-aggression pact among member States; elaboration of specific measures to promote the balanced and gradual reduction of armed forces, armaments and military budgets; and consideration of specific measures and mechanisms for crisis management and peace-keeping in the subregion. The meeting is also expected to review the latest geopolitical and security-related developments in the subregion, including the situations in Angola, Rwanda and Zaire, which have attracted international attention and various levels of United Nations involvement. At its most recent meeting in Bujumbura in March this year, the Committee called on all member States to adhere to existing international agreements on disarmament and arms limitation.

The Office for Disarmament Affairs provides secretariat support for the Committee. Sammy Kum Buo of that Office serves as Secretary of the Committee. The Secretary-General is expected to submit a report to the forty-eighth session of the General Assembly on the work of the Committee during 1993.

The membership of the Committee consists of the 11 States members of the Economic Community of Central African States. They are Angola, Burundi, Cameroon, Central African Republic, Chad, Congo, Equatorial Guinea, Gabon, Rwanda, Sao Tome and Principe and Zaire. The current Bureau of the Committee is as follows: Burundi, Chairman; Gabon, First Vice-Chairman; Congo, Second Vice-Chairman; Chad, Rapporteur.

DC/2446 - 7 October 1993

STATES OF CENTRAL AFRICAN SUBREGION ADOPT NON-AGGRESSION PACT

NEW YORK, 7 October (Off ice for Disarmament Affairs) -- A Non-Aggression Pact among the 11 member States of the Economic Community of Central African States (ECCAS) has been unanimously adopted at the Ministerial Meeting of the Standing Advisory Committee on Security Questions in Central Africa, held in Libreville, Gabon.

The ECCAS was established by the Secretary-General on 28 May 1992, in response to a General Assembly decision of 6 December 1991, taken in resolution 46/37 B.

The key paragraphs of the Pact include the commitment of the Committee's 11 members (Angola, Burundi, Cameroon, Central African Republic, Chad, Congo, Equatorial Guinea, Gabon, Rwanda, Sao Tome and Principe and Zaire) not to resort to the threat or use of force in inter-state relations, and to respect the territorial integrity and independence of other member States in accordance with the Charters of the United Nations and the Organization of African Unity (OAU). Each member State also pledges not to commit, encourage or support acts of hostility or aggression against the territorial integrity and independence of other member States and to prevent such acts from being carried out by foreigners on their territory. Should differences occur among member States, the Pact provides for recourse to the relevant mechanisms of ECCAS, the OAU and the United Nations, as appropriate.

The Pact will come into force when ratified by seven of its 11 members.

The Libreville meeting also authorizes the Bureau of the Committee to play a more active political role in subregional crises and to undertake missions of solidarity to countries in the subregion that were in conflict, in order to express the Committee's support for a peaceful and speedy resolution of the conflict.

The Committee also agreed that its member States should consider possible ways and means of reducing their armed forces, military budgets and equipment. It decided that member States should forward appropriate data on their military spending and acquisitions to the United Nations Register on Conventional Arms and should sign and/or ratify multilateral arms regulation and disarmament agreements within 18 months.

The 11 member States further agreed to continue and to strengthen the process of democratization in their respective countries and to respect human rights in order to ensure peace, stability and development in the subregion.

At the opening ceremony of the Ministerial Meeting, the special representative of the Secretary-General, Hassen Fodha, observed that the Committee was an instrument of much promise in the building of confidence, security and stability in the subregion.

During the meeting, the Committee elected a new Bureau as follows: President: Gabon; First Vice-President: Congo;

Second Vice-president: Angola; Rapporteur: Zaire.

The next Ministerial Meeting of the Committee is scheduled for Brazzaville (Congo) in six months.

DC/2460 - 28 March 1994

STANDING ADVISORY COMMITTEE ON SECURITY QUESTIONS IN CENTRAL AFRICA TO MEET IN YAOUNDE, CAMEROON, 4 - 8 APRIL

NEW YORK, 28 March (Centre for Disarmament Affairs) - - The Standing Advisory Committee on Security Questions in Central Africa will hold its fourth ministerial meeting from 4 to 8 April 1994 in Yaounde, Cameroon.

The Committee's last ministerial session was held in September 1993 at Libreville, Gabon. At that session, the Committee unanimously adopted a non-aggression pact among its 11 member States - - Angola, Burundi, Cameroon, Chad, Central African Republic, Congo, Equatorial Guinea, Gabon, Rwanda, Sao Tome and Principe and Zaire - - and empowered its Bureau to play a more active political role in conflict resolution in the subregion.

Since the last meeting of the Committee, crisis situations have persisted in many countries, particularly Angola, Burundi, Congo, Rwanda and Zaire. At its upcoming meeting, the Committee is expected to examine the geopolitical and security situation in central Africa, including the consideration of ways and means for the peaceful resolution of the conflicts in the subregion, as well as to exchange views on subregional collective defence, confidence-building measures and preventive diplomacy. The Committee is also expected to continue to examine the creation of an inter-State permanent staff for crisis management and peace-keeping in the subregion of central Africa.

The establishment of the Committee was announced on 28 May 1992 by Secretary-General Boutros Boutros-Ghali, pursuant to General Assembly resolution 46/37 B of 6 December 1991. By that resolution, the Assembly welcomed the initiative taken by the Member States of the Economic Community of Central African States to create, under the auspices of the United Nations, a Standing Advisory Committee on Security Questions in Central Africa and requested the Secretary-General to establish the Committee.

The objective of the Committee is to develop confidence-building measures, pursue arms limitation and promote economic development in the subregion. The Committee meets at the level of defence and foreign ministers, who are assisted by appropriate experts, such as senior military and civilian officials. Discussions also take place at the level of Heads of State during the Summit meetings of the Economic Community of Central African States.

The Bureau of the Committee is currently composed as follows: President, Minister of Defence and Security of Gabon; First Vice-President, Minister for Foreign Affairs of Congo; Second Vice-President, Minister for Foreign Affairs of Angola; Rapporteur-General, Zaire.

Sammy Kum Buo, Senior Political Affairs Officer of the United Nations Centre for Disarmament Affairs, serves as Secretary of the Committee.

STANDING ADVISORY COMMITTEE ON SECURITY QUESTIONS IN CENTRAL AFRICA TO HOLD SIXTH MINISTERIAL MEETING IN BRAZZAVILLE, 20-24 MARCH

NEW YORK, 14 March (Department of Political Affairs) -- The 11 member States of the United Nations Standing Advisory Committee on Security Questions in Central Africa are scheduled to hold their sixth Ministerial meeting in Brazzaville, Congo, from 20 to 24 March.

The Committee is made up of Angola, Burundi, Cameroon, Central African Republic, Chad, Congo, Equatorial Guinea, Gabon, Rwanda, Sao Tome and Principe and Zaire. Its establishment was announced by Secretary-General Boutros Boutros-Ghali on 28 May 1992 in response to a General Assembly resolution for the purpose of preventing the outbreak and escalation of crisis and conflict in the subregion through confidence-building measures, arms restraint and disarmament. The Committee meets as appropriate at the level of military and civilian experts, Ministers of Defence and of Foreign Affairs or Heads of State. It is serviced by the Centre for Disarmament Affairs in the Department of Political Affairs.

At its fifth Ministerial meeting held in Yaounde, Cameroon, last September, the Committee initialed a non-aggression pact unanimously adopted among its member States at its third Ministerial meeting in Libreville, Gabon, in September 1993. And it began consideration of sources of internal crises and conflicts and the elaboration of a protocol on mutual defence assistance among member States. Committee members also agreed to set aside specialized units in their respective armed forces for possible deployment in the United Nations, the Organization of African Unity

(OAU) or other peace-keeping operations in the subregion.

Committee members view the upcoming meeting as an opportunity to commemorate the fiftieth anniversary of the United Nations in the subregion by highlighting the Organization's role and current efforts in the maintenance of peace and security in central Africa. Thus, the agenda of the meeting features, among other items, an overview of the geo-political and security situation in the subregion with emphasis on concrete efforts towards the peaceful resolution of the conflicts in Angola, Burundi and Rwanda, and the various ways and means of consolidating inter-State and subregional cooperation in responding to the ensuing refugee and security-related repercussions.

At a panel discussion, leading African and international experts will highlight the contribution of the media in the peaceful resolution of crises in central Africa as well as the role of external Powers and the United Nations Security Council. Committee members are also expected to continue consultations on the consolidation of the agreement reached on the non-aggression pact and its formal signing later this year by Heads of State.

The Ministerial meeting, which will include, Defence and Foreign Affairs Ministers from the subregion, will be inaugurated on 23 March by Prime Minister Yhombi Opango of Congo, and will be preceded by a three-day high-level experts' session. The Secretary-General is expected to be represented.

Speaking recently on the Committee, Secretary-General Boutros Boutros-Ghali emphasized that the commitment made by the States of the central African subregion to renounce the use of force as a policy option in their relations and to seek constructive and practical measures to strengthen confidence and cooperation

among States was a significant development in the relentless search for durable peace and security which requires the full support and encouragement of the international community. It has been noted that the subregion has been plagued in recent times by political turbulence and spiralling armed conflicts in Angola, Burundi, Chad, Congo, Rwanda and Zaire.

Officers of the Committee are: President, Cameroon; First Vice-President, Congo; Second Vice-President, Angola; Rapporteur, Zaire. According to its practice, it is expected that the Committee will elect new officers for a one-year term of office. Sammy Kum Buo, Senior Political Affairs Officer with the Centre for Disarmament Affairs, serves as Secretary to the Committee.

SG/SM/5942 - 29 March 1996

SECRETARY-GENERAL ANNOUNCES ESTABLISHMENT OF TRUST FUND TO PROMOTE CONFIDENCE-BUILDING IN CENTRAL AFRICA

Secretary-General Boutros Boutros-Ghali has announced the establishment of a trust fund to finance activities aimed at promoting confidence-building measures and preventing further armed conflicts in one of Africa's most turbulent subregions. Known formally as the Trust Fund for the United Nations Standing Advisory Committee on Security Questions in Central Africa, it was set up at the request of the General Assembly, under its resolution 50/71/B of 12 December 1995, to raise additional resources on a voluntary basis for the implementation of the programme of work of the Committee.

The Standing Advisory Committee on Security Questions in Central Africa was established by the Secretary-General in May 1992 in response to General Assembly resolution 46/37/B of 6 December 1991. Its purpose is to promote confidence-building measures, arm restraint and disarmament in the subregion. The 11 members of the Committee are Angola, Burundi, Cameroon, Central African Republic, Chad, Congo, Equatorial Guinea, Gabon, Rwanda, Sao Tome and Principe and Zaire.

Members of the Committee have decided to establish units specializing in peace operations within their respective armed forces and to participate in such operations within the framework either of the United Nations or the Organization of African Unity (OAU). The General Assembly has welcomed the decision and called for voluntary contributions to finance training programmes for the peace units.

The Trust Fund will also be used to support efforts by the Committee to control the illicit transfer and proliferation of small arms in the subregion, to promote arms restraint and transparency in military acquisitions through the establishment of a sub-regional register of conventional armaments, to foster inter-State cooperation on security matters and to contribute to the peaceful resolution of existing conflicts in the subregion, in particular those in Angola and in the countries of the Great Lakes area.

Ministers of Defence and/or Foreign Affairs of the 11 Member States of the Committee are scheduled to meet in Yaounde, Cameroon, from 18 to 19 April to review the geo-political and security situation in the subregion and to prepare for a summit conference of their heads of State and government, which is also expected to take place in Yaounde, in July. A key item on the summit agenda will be the formal signature of the Non-Aggression Pact, designed to prevent inter-State conflict and contribute to confidence-building in the subregion.

The Secretary of the Committee is Sammy Kum Buo, a Senior Political Affairs Officer in the Centre for Disarmament Affairs, Department of Political Affairs.

SG/SM/6159 - 14 February 1997

SECRETARY-GENERAL MEETS WITH CONGO'S FOREIGN MINISTER, CURRENT CHAIR OF COMMITTEE ON CENTRAL AFRICAN SECURITY

The following statement was issued today by the Spokesman for Secretary-General Kofi Annan:

The Secretary-General met on 12 February with the Foreign Minister of the Congo, Destin-Arsene Tsaty-Boungou, who is the current Chairman of the Standing Advisory Committee on Security Questions in Central Africa created by the General Assembly two years ago. They reviewed the work of the Committee with regard to the situation in the Great Lakes region, as well as various initiatives taken by Member States in this context.

They agreed on the need to maintain the impetus in the search for peace in the region and to call a regional conference on democratic institutions and peace in Central Africa, to be held in Brazzaville from 30 March to 3 April 1997, to which the political leaders, the opposition members and the civil society of the countries of the region would be invited. They called on the international community to help ensure the success of the conference. They also discussed the situation in Zaire and the various peace initiatives taken thereon, as well as the situation in Burundi. Finally, the Foreign Minister spoke of the next presidential elections in his country, which are to be held in August 1997.

United Nations Security Council Resolutions
relating to the establishment of peace operations in central Africa

S/RES/143 (ONUC)

The Security Council,

Considering the report of the Secretary-General 1/ on a request for United Nations action in relation to the Republic of the Congo,

Considering the request for military assistance addressed to the Secretary-General by the President and the Prime Minister of the Republic of the Congo (S/4382),

1. Calls upon the Government of Belgium to withdraw its troops from the territory of the Republic of the Congo;

2. Decides to authorize the Secretary-General to take the necessary steps, in consultation with the Government of the Republic of the Congo, to provide the Government with such military assistance as may be necessary until, through the efforts of the Congolese Government with the technical assistance of the United Nations, the national security forces may be able, in the opinion of the Government, to meet fully their tasks;

3. Requests the Secretary-General to report to the Security Council as appropriate.

873rd meeting
14 July 1960

1/ *Official Records of the Security Council, Fifteenth Year,* 873rd meeting, paras. 18-29.

S/RES/626 (UNAVEM I)

The Security Council,

Noting the decision of Angola and Cuba to conclude a bilateral agreement on 22 December 1988 for the redeployment to the north and the staged and total withdrawal of Cuban troops from Angola, according to the agreed time-table,

Considering the request submitted to the Secretary-General by Angola and Cuba in letters dated 17 December 1988 (S/20336 and S/20337),

Having considered the report of the Secretary-General dated 17 December 1988 (S/20338),

1. Approves the report of the Secretary-General and the recommendations therein;

2. Decides to establish under its authority a United Nations Angola Verification Mission and requests the Secretary-General to take the necessary steps to this effect in accordance with his aforementioned report;

3. Also decides that the Mission shall be established for a period of thirty-one months;

4. Further decides that the arrangements for the establishment of the Mission shall enter into force as soon as the tripartite agreement between Angola, Cuba and South Africa on the one hand, and the bilateral agreement between Angola and Cuba on the other, are signed;

5. Requests the Secretary-General to report to the Security Council immediately after the signature of the agreements referred to in paragraph 4 and to keep the

Council fully informed of further developments.

2834th meeting
20 December 1988

S/RES/696 (UNAVEM II)

The Security Council,

Welcoming the decision of the Government of the People's Republic of Angola and the National Union for the Total Independence of Angola to conclude the Peace Accords for Angola,

Stressing the importance it attaches to the signing of the Peace Accords and to the fulfilment by the parties in good faith of the obligations contained therein,

Stressing also the importance of all States refraining from taking any actions which could undermine the agreements mentioned above and contributing to their implementation, as well as respecting fully the independence, sovereignty and territorial integrity of Angola,

Noting with satisfaction the decision taken by the Government of the People's Republic of Angola and the Government of the Republic of Cuba to complete the withdrawal, ahead of Schedule, of all Cuban troops from Angola by 25 May 1991 (S/22644, annex),

Considering the request submitted to the Secretary-General by the Minister for Foreign Affairs of the People's Republic of Angola in his letter dated 8 May 1991 (S/22609),

Having considered the report of the Secretary-General of 20 and 29 May 1991 (S/22627 and Add.l),

Taking into account that the mandate of the United Nations Angola Verification Mission established by Council resolution 626 (1988) of 20 December 1988 expires on 22 July 1991,

1. Approves the report of the Secretary-General of 20 and 29 May 1991 (S/22627 and Add.1) and the recommendations therein;

2. Decides accordingly to entrust a new mandate to the United Nations Angola Verification Mission (henceforth United Nations Angola Verification Mission II) as proposed by the Secretary-General in line with the Peace Accords for Angola, and requests the Secretary-General to take the necessary steps to this effect;

3. Also decides to establish the United Nations Angola Verification Mission II for a period of seventeen months from the date of adoption of the present resolution in order to accomplish the objectives stated in the report of the Secretary-General;

4. Requests the Secretary-General to report to the Security Council immediately after the signature of the Peace Accords and to keep the Council fully informed of further developments.

2991st meeting
30 May 1991

S/RES/ 846 (UNOMUR)

The Security Council,

Reaffirming its resolution 812 (1993) of 12 March 1993,

Taking note of the interim report of the Secretary-General dated 20 May 1993 (S/25810 and Add.1),

Also taking note of the requests of the Governments of Rwanda and Uganda for the deployment of United Nations observers along their common border as a temporary confidence-building measure (S/25355, S/25356, S/25797),

Emphasizing the need to prevent the resumption of fighting in Rwanda that could have adverse consequences on the situation in Rwanda and on international peace and security,

Stressing the need for a negotiated political solution, in the framework of the agreements to be signed by the parties in Arusha, in order to put an end to the conflict in Rwanda,

Paying tribute to the efforts of the Organization of African Unity (OAU) and the Government of the United Republic of Tanzania to promote such a political solution,

Taking note of the joint request of the Government of Rwanda and the Rwandese Patriotic Front (RPF) concerning the establishment of a neutral international force in Rwanda (S/25951),

Stressing the importance of the ongoing negotiations in Arusha between the Government of Rwanda and the RPF, and expressing its readiness to consider assistance to the OAU in the implementation of the agreements as soon as they are signed,

1. Welcomes with appreciation the report of the Secretary-General (S/25810 and Add.1);

2. Decides to establish the United Nations Observer Mission Uganda -Rwanda (UNOMUR) that will be deployed on the Ugandan side of the border, for an initial period of six months, as set out in the report of the Secretary-General (S/25810 and Add.1), and subject to review every six months;

3. Decides that UNOMUR shall monitor the Uganda/Rwanda border to verify that no military assistance reaches Rwanda, focus being put primarily in this regard on transit or transport, by roads or tracks which could accommodate vehicles, of lethal weapons and ammunition across the border, as well as any other material which could be of military use;

4. Requests the Secretary-General to conclude with the Government of Uganda, before the full deployment of UNOMUR, a status of mission agreement including the safety, cooperation and support the Government of Uganda will provide to UNOMUR;

5. Approves the dispatching of an advance party within fifteen days of the adoption of this resolution or as soon as possible after the conclusion of the status of mission agreement and the full deployment within thirty days of the arrival of the advance party;

6. Urges the Government of Rwanda and the RPF strictly to respect the rules of international humanitarian law;

7. Further urges the Government of Rwanda and the RPF to refrain from any action that could contribute to tension;

8. Welcomes the decision of the Secretary-General to support the peace efforts of the OAU by putting two military experts at its disposal with a view to assisting the Neutral Military Observer Group (NMOG), in particular through logistic expertise to help expedite deployment of the enlarged NMOG to Rwanda;

9. Urges the Government of Rwanda and the RPF to conclude quickly a comprehensive peace agreement;

10. Requests the Secretary-General to report to the Council on the results of the Arusha peace talks;

11. **Further requests** the Secretary-General to report on the contribution the United Nations could make to assist the OAU in the implementation of the above-mentioned agreement and to begin contingency planning in the event that the Council decides such a contribution is needed;

12. **Also requests** the Secretary-General to report to the Council on the implementation of the present resolution within sixty days of the deployment of UNOMUR;

13. **Decides** to remain actively seized of the matter.

3244th meeting
22 June 1993

S/RES/872 (UNAMIR)

.The Security Council,

Reaffirming its resolutions 812 (1993) of 12 March 1993 and 846 (1993) of 22 June 1993,

Reaffirming also its resolution 868 (1993) of 29 September 1993 on the security of United Nations operations,

Having considered the report of the Secretary-General of 24 September 1993 (S/26488 and Add.1),

Welcoming the signing of the Arusha Peace Agreement (including its Protocols) on 4 August 1993 and **urging** the parties to continue to comply fully with it,

Noting the conclusion of the Secretary-General that in order to enable the United Nations to carry out its mandate successfully and effectively, the full cooperation of the parties with one another and with the Organization is required,

Stressing the urgency of the deployment of an international neutral force in Rwanda, as underlined both by the Government of the Republic of Rwanda and by the Rwandese Patriotic Front and as reaffirmed by their joint delegation in New York,

Paying tribute to the role played by the Organization of African Unity (OAU) and by the Government of the United Republic of Tanzania in the conclusion of the Arusha Peace Agreement,

Resolved that the United Nations should, at the request of the parties and under peaceful conditions with the full cooperation of all the parties, make its full contribution to the implementation of the Arusha Peace Agreement,

1. **Welcomes** the report of the Secretary-General (S/26488);

2. **Decides** to establish a peace-keeping operation under the name "United Nations Assistance Mission for Rwanda" (UNAMIR) for a period of six months subject to the proviso that it will be extended beyond the initial ninety days only upon a review by the Council based on a report from the Secretary-General as to whether or not substantive progress has been made towards the implementation of the Arusha Peace Agreement;

3. **Decides** that, drawing from the Secretary-General's recommendations, UNAMIR shall have the following mandate:

(a) To contribute to the security of the city of Kigali _inter alia_ within a weapons-secure area established by the parties in and around the city;

(b) To monitor observance of the cease-fire agreement, which calls for the establishment of cantonment and assembly zones and the demarcation of the new demilitarized zone and other demilitarization procedures;

(c) To monitor the security situation during the final period of the transitional government's mandate, leading up to the elections;

(d) To assist with mine clearance, primarily through training programmes;

(e) To investigate at the request of the parties or on its own initiative instances of alleged non-compliance with the provisions of the Arusha Peace Agreement relating to the integration of the armed forces, and pursue any such instances with the parties responsible and report thereon as appropriate to the Secretary-General;

(f) To monitor the process of repatriation of Rwandese refugees and resettlement of displaced persons to verify that it is carried out in a safe and orderly manner;

(g) To assist in the coordination of humanitarian assistance activities in conjunction with relief operations;

(h) To investigate and report on incidents regarding the activities of the gendarmerie and police;

4. Approves the Secretary-General's proposal that the United Nations Observer Mission Uganda-Rwanda (UNOMUR) established by resolution 846 (1993) should be integrated within UNAMIR;

5. Welcomes the efforts and the cooperation of the OAU in helping to implement the Arusha Peace Agreement, in particular the integration of the Neutral Military Observer Group (NMOG II) within UNAMIR;

6. Further approves the Secretary-General's proposal that the deployment and withdrawal of UNAMIR should be carried out in stages and notes in this connection that UNAMIR's mandate, if extended, is expected to terminate following national elections and the installation of a new government in Rwanda, events which are scheduled to occur by October 1995, but no later than December 1995;

7. Authorizes the Secretary-General, in this context, to deploy the first contingent, at the level specified by the Secretary-General's report, to Kigali for an initial period of six months, in the shortest possible time, which, when fully in place, will permit the establishment of the transitional institutions and implementation of the other relevant provisions of the Arusha Peace Agreement;

8. Invites the Secretary-General, in the context of the report referred to in paragraph 2 above, also to report on the progress of UNAMIR following its initial deployment, and resolves to review as appropriate, on the basis of that report and as part of the review referred to in paragraph 2 above, the requirement for further deployments in the scale and composition recommended by the Secretary-General in his report (S/26488);

9. Invites the Secretary-General to consider ways of reducing the total maximum strength of UNAMIR, in particular through phased deployment without thereby affecting the capacity of UNAMIR to carry out its mandate, and requests the Secretary-General in planning and executing the phased deployment of UNAMIR to seek economies and to report regularly on what is achieved in this regard;

10. Welcomes the intention of the Secretary-General to appoint a Special Representative who would lead UNAMIR in the field and exercise authority over all its elements;

11. Urges the parties to implement the Arusha Peace Agreement in good faith;

12. Also requests the Secretary-General to conclude expeditiously an agreement on the status of the operation, and all personnel engaged in the operation in Rwanda, to come into force as near as

possible to the outset of the operation and no later than thirty days after the adoption of this resolution;

13. Demands that the parties take all appropriate steps to ensure the security and safety of the operation and personnel engaged in the operation;

14. Urges Member States, United Nations agencies and non-governmental organizations to provide and intensify their economic, financial and humanitarian assistance in favour of the Rwandese population and of the democratization process in Rwanda;

15. Decides to remain actively seized of the matter.

3288th meeting
5 October 1993

S/RES/915 (UNASOG)

The Security Council,

Recalling its resolution 910 (1994) of 14 April 1994,

Welcoming the signing on 4 April 1994 at Surt (Libya), by the representatives of the Republic of Chad on the one hand and of the Great Socialist People's Libyan Arab Jamahiriya on the other hand, of the agreement relating to the implementation of the Judgment of the International Court of Justice of 3 February 1994,

Taking note of the letter dated 6 April 1994 from the Permanent Representative of the Libyan Arab Jamahiriya to the United Nations addressed to the Secretary-General (S/1994/402) and the letter dated 13 April 1994 from the Permanent Representative of Chad to the United Nations addressed to the Secretary-General (S/1994/424), and the annexes thereto,

Noting that the agreement signed at Surt (Libya) provides that United Nations observers shall be present during all the Libyan withdrawal operations and shall establish that the withdrawal is actually effected,

Determined to assist the parties in implementing the Judgment of the International Court of Justice concerning their territorial dispute and thereby to help promote peaceful relations between them, in keeping with the principles and purposes of the Charter of the United Nations,

Having examined the report of the Secretary-General dated 27 April 1994 (S/1994/512),

A

1. Takes note with appreciation of the report of the Secretary-General on the implementation of the provisions of article 1 of the above-mentioned agreement (S/1994/512);

2. Decides to establish the United Nations Aouzou Strip Observer Group (UNASOG) and authorizes the deployment for a single period of up to forty days, starting from the date of the present resolution, of nine United Nations observers and six support staff to observe the implementation of the agreement signed on 4 April 1994 at Surt (Libya) in accordance with the recommendations of the Secretary-General (S/1994/512) and in accordance with paragraph 9 of resolution 907 (1994) of 29 March 1994;

3. Calls upon the parties to cooperate fully with the Secretary-General in verifying implementation of the provisions of the agreement of 4 April 1994 and, in particular, to grant UNASOG freedom of movement and all the services it requires in order to fulfil its functions;

B

Recognizing that UNASOG will need to travel to the Libyan Arab Jamahiriya by air and that this will require an exemption from the provisions of paragraph 4 of resolution 748 (1992) of 31 March 1992, and acting, in this respect, under Chapter VII of the Charter of the United Nations,

4. Decides that paragraph 4 of resolution 748 (1992) of 31 March 1992 shall not apply in respect of aircraft flying to or from the Libyan Arab Jamahiriya for the purpose of conveying UNASOG;

5. Requests the Secretary-General to inform the Committee established pursuant to resolution 748 (1992) of flights made to or from the Libyan Arab Jamahiriya in accordance with the present resolution;

C

6. Invites the Secretary-General to keep it informed as appropriate of the progress of the mission and to report at the time of its completion;

7. Decides to remain seized of the matter.

3373rd meeting
4 May 1994

S/RES/929 (Operation "Turquoise")

The Security Council,

Reaffirming all its previous resolutions on the situation in Rwanda, in particular its resolutions 912 (1994) of 21 April 1994, 918 (1994) of 17 May 1994 and 925 (1994) of 8 June 1994, which set out the mandate and force level of the United Nations Assistance Mission for Rwanda (UNAMIR),

Determined to contribute to the resumption of the process of political settlement under the Arusha Peace Agreement and encouraging the Secretary-General and his Special Representative for Rwanda to continue and redouble their efforts at the national, regional and international levels to promote these objectives,

Stressing the importance of the cooperation of all parties for the fulfilment of the objectives of the United Nations in Rwanda,

Having considered the letter of the Secretary-General of 19 June 1994 (S/1994/728),

Taking into account the time needed to gather the necessary resources for the effective deployment of UNAMIR, as expanded in resolutions 918 (1994) and 925 (1994),

Noting the offer by Member States to cooperate with the Secretary-General towards the fulfilment of the objectives of the United Nations in Rwanda (S/1994/734), and stressing the strictly humanitarian character of this operation which shall be conducted in an impartial and neutral fashion, and shall not constitute an interposition force between the parties,

Welcoming the cooperation between the United Nations, the Organization of African Unity (OAU) and neighbouring States to bring peace to Rwanda,

Deeply concerned by the continuation of systematic and widespread killings of the civilian population in Rwanda,

Recognizing that the current situation in Rwanda constitutes a unique case which demands an urgent response by the international community,

Determining that the magnitude of the humanitarian crisis in Rwanda constitutes a threat to peace and security in the region,

1. Welcomes the Secretary-General's letter dated 19 June 1994 (S/1994/728) and agrees that a multinational operation may be set up for humanitarian purposes in Rwanda until UNAMIR is brought up to the necessary strength;

2. Welcomes also the offer by Member States (S/1994/734) to cooperate with the Secretary-General in order to achieve the objectives of the United Nations in Rwanda through the establishment of a temporary operation under national command and control aimed at contributing, in an impartial way, to the security and protection of displaced persons, refugees and civilians at risk in Rwanda, on the understanding that the costs of implementing the offer will be borne by the Member States concerned;

3. Acting under Chapter VII of the Charter of the United Nations, authorizes the Member States cooperating with the Secretary-General to conduct the operation referred to in paragraph 2 above using all necessary means to achieve the humanitarian objectives set out in subparagraphs 4 (a) and (b) of resolution 925 (1994);

4. Decides that the mission of Member States cooperating with the Secretary-General will be limited to a period of two months following the adoption of the present resolution, unless the Secretary-General determines at an earlier date that the expanded UNAMIR is able to carry out its mandate;

5. Commends the offers already made by Member States of troops for the expanded UNAMIR;

6. Calls upon all Member States to respond urgently to the Secretary-General's request for resources, including logistical support, in order to enable expanded UNAMIR to fulfil its mandate effectively as soon as possible and requests the Secretary-General to identify and coordinate the supply of the essential equipment required by troops committed to the expanded UNAMIR;

7. Welcomes, in this respect, the offers already made by Member States of equipment for troop contributors to UNAMIR and calls on other Members to offer such support, including the possibility of comprehensive provision of equipment to specific troop contributors, to speed UNAMIR's expanded force deployment;

8. Requests Member States cooperating with the Secretary-General to coordinate closely with UNAMIR and also requests the Secretary-General to set up appropriate mechanisms to this end;

9. Demands that all parties to the conflict and others concerned immediately bring to an end all killings of civilian populations in areas under their control and allow Member States cooperating with the Secretary-General to implement fully the mission set forth in paragraph 3 above;

10. Requests the States concerned and the Secretary-General, as appropriate, to report to the Council on a regular basis, the first such report to be made no later than fifteen days after the adoption of this resolution, on the implementation of this operation and the progress made towards the fulfilment of the objectives referred to in paragraphs 2 and 3 above;

11. Also requests the Secretary-General to report on the progress made towards completing the deployment of the expanded UNAMIR within the framework of the report due no later than 9 August 1994 under paragraph 17 of resolution 925 (1994), as well as on progress towards the resumption of the process of political settlement under the Arusha Peace Agreement;

12. **Decides** to remain actively seized of the matter.

3392nd meeting
22 June 1994

S/RES/976 (UNAVEM III)

The Security Council,

Reaffirming its resolution 696 (1991) of 30 May 1991 and all subsequent relevant resolutions,

Having considered the report of the Secretary-General dated 1 February 1995 (S/1995/97 and Add.1),

Reaffirming its commitment to preserve the unity and territorial integrity of Angola,

Welcoming the signing of the Lusaka Protocol of 20 November 1994 (S/1994/1441, annex) as a major step towards the establishment of peace and stability in Angola,

Reiterating the importance it attaches to the full implementation of the "Acordos de Paz" (S/22609, annex), the Lusaka Protocol and relevant Security Council resolutions,

Noting the schedule for implementation set forth in the Lusaka Protocol, in particular the need for the Government of Angola and UNITA to provide all relevant military data to the United Nations, to allow freedom of movement and free circulation of goods, and to begin limited disengagement where forces are in contact,

Welcoming the maintenance of a cease-fire which has been generally holding,

Welcoming also the progress made in meetings of the Angolan Armed Forces and UNITA Chiefs of Staff on 10 January 1995 in Chipipa and on 2 to 3 February 1995 in Waco Kungo,

Further welcoming the deployment of United Nations Angola Verification Mission (UNAVEM II) observer forces, and the contributions of Member States to this mission,

Welcoming the offer from the Government of Angola to provide substantial contributions in-kind to United Nations peace-keeping operations in Angola as set out in "Costs of the Implementation of the Lusaka Protocol" (S/1994/1451),

Deeply concerned that the implementation of the Lusaka Protocol has fallen behind schedule,

Stressing the need for the President of Angola, Mr. Jose Eduardo dos Santos, and the leader of UNITA, Dr. Jonas Savimbi, to meet without delay with a view to building the necessary political momentum for the successful implementation of the Lusaka Protocol,

Welcoming the Ministerial delegation of the Organization of African Unity (OAU) to the Security Council to participate in its consideration of the situation in Angola,

1. **Authorizes** the establishment of a peace-keeping operation, UNAVEM III to assist the parties in restoring peace and achieving national reconciliation in Angola on the basis of the "Acordos de Paz", the Lusaka Protocol and relevant Security Council resolutions, as outlined in part IV of the report of the Secretary-General dated 1 February 1995, with an initial mandate until 8 August 1995 and with a maximum deployment of 7,000 military personnel, in addition to the 350 military observers and 260 police observers mentioned in the Secretary-General's report, with an appropriate number of international and local staff;

2. Urges the expeditious deployment of the military and police observers to monitor the cease-fire;

3. Authorizes the immediate deployment of such planning and support elements as are needed to prepare for the deployment of peace-keeping forces provided that the Secretary-General remains satisfied that an effective cease-fire and effective joint cease-fire monitoring mechanisms are in place, and that both parties are allowing the free and safe flow of humanitarian assistance throughout the country, and authorizes the subsequent deployment of such additional elements as are necessary to establish operational quartering areas for UNITA forces;

4. Decides that the deployment of infantry units will take place on the basis of a report from the Secretary-General to the Security Council that the conditions contained in paragraph 32 of the Secretary-General's report, inter alia, effective cessation of hostilities, provision of all relevant military data, and designation of all quartering areas, have been met, provided the Council does not decide otherwise;

5. Stresses the importance it attaches to the expeditious establishment of a well-coordinated and comprehensive mine clearance programme in Angola as set out in the Secretary-General's report dated 1 February 1995, and requests him to inform the Council of progress in its implementation;

6. Endorses the Secretary-General's view set out in his report (S/1995/97 and Add.1) as to the need for UNAVEM III to have an effective information capability, including a United Nations radio station to be established in consultation with the Government of Angola;

7. Requests the Secretary-General to inform the Council monthly of progress in the deployment of UNAVEM III and in

implementation of the Lusaka Protocol, including the maintenance of an effective cease-fire, free access by UNAVEM III to all areas of Angola, free flow of humanitarian assistance throughout Angola and compliance by both the Government of Angola and by UNITA with their obligations under the Lusaka Protocol, and further requests the Secretary-General to submit to the Council a complete report by 15 July 1995;

8. Welcomes the Secretary-General's intention to include human rights specialists in the political component of UNAVEM III to observe the implementation of the provisions related to national reconciliation;

9. Expresses its intention to review the role of the United Nations in Angola should the Secretary-General report that the cooperation required from the parties is substantially delayed or not forthcoming;

10. Declares its intention to conclude the mission of UNAVEM III when the objectives of the Lusaka Protocol have been achieved in accordance with the schedule attached to the Lusaka Protocol and with the expectation of its completion by February 1997;

11. Welcomes the substantial contributions of the Member States, United Nations agencies and non-governmental organizations to meet the humanitarian needs of the Angolan people and encourages additional substantial contributions;

12. Reaffirms the obligation of all States to implement fully the provisions of paragraph 19 of resolution 864 (1993), and calls upon the Government of Angola and UNITA during UNAVEM III's presence in Angola to cease any acquisition of arms and war materiel, as agreed upon in the "Acordos de Paz", and to devote their resources instead to priority humanitarian and social needs;

13. Calls upon the Government of Angola to conclude no later than 20 March 1995 an agreement with the United Nations on the Status of Forces;

14. Encourages the Secretary-General to pursue urgently the offer of direct assistance by the Government of Angola to UNAVEM III, to reflect this as appropriate in the Status of Forces Agreement referred to in paragraph 13 above, and to explore with the Government of Angola and UNITA possibilities for substantial additional assistance related to peace-keeping and to report to the Council on the results of these explorations;

15. Urges Member States to respond positively to the request made to them by the Secretary-General to contribute personnel, equipment and other resources to UNAVEM III in order to facilitate its early deployment;

16. Demands that all concerned in Angola take the necessary measures to ensure the safety and freedom of movement of United Nations and other personnel deployed under UNAVEM III;

17. Welcomes the presence of the OAU Ministerial delegation and notes, in this connection, the need for continued cooperation between the United Nations and the OAU in the promotion of peace and security in Angola and the contribution which regional organizations can make to crisis management and conflict resolution;

18. Decides to remain actively seized of the matter.

3499th meeting
8 February 1995

S/RES/1118 (MONUA)

The Security Council,

Reaffirming its resolution 696 (1991) of 30 May 1991 and all subsequent resolutions,

Reaffirming also its commitment to the unity and territorial integrity of Angola,

Recognizing the successful contribution of UNAVEM III to the restoration of peace and the process of national reconciliation on the basis of the "Acordos de Paz" (S/22609, annex), the Lusaka Protocol (S/1994/1441, annex) and relevant Security Council resolutions,

Recognizing also that the formation of the Government of National Unity and Reconciliation (GURN) provides a strong basis for the process of national reconciliation,

Emphasizing the need for the Government of Angola and the Uniao Nacional para a Independencia Total de Angola (UNITA) to implement without further delay the remaining political and military tasks of the peace process,

Expressing its concern about the recent increase in tensions, especially in the northeastern provinces, and the attacks by UNITA on UNAVEM III posts and personnel,

Reiterating that the ultimate responsibility for the completion of the peace process rests with the Angolan people themselves,

Having considered the report of the Secretary-General of 5 June 1997 (S/1997/438),

1. Welcomes the recommendations contained in the report of the Secretary-General of 5 June 1997;

2. Decides to establish, as of 1 July, the United Nations Observer Mission in Angola (MONUA) with the objectives, mandate, and organizational structure recommended by the Secretary-General in section VII of his report of 5 June 1997;

3. Also decides, with the expectation of full completion of the mission by 1 February 1998, that the initial mandate of MONUA will extend until 31 October 1997, and requests the Secretary-General to report on the situation by 15 August 1997;

4. Further decides that MONUA will assume responsibility for all components and assets of UNAVEM III remaining in Angola, including formed military units, to deploy as appropriate until they are withdrawn;

5. Requests the Secretary-General to continue to take into account the situation on the ground and progress in completing the remaining relevant aspects of the peace process in implementing the scheduled withdrawal of United Nations military units, and to report thereon in the context of the review requested in paragraph 3;

6. Calls upon the Government of Angola to apply mutatis mutandis to MONUA and its members the Agreement concluded on 3 May 1995 between the United Nations and the Government of Angola on the Status of the United Nations Peacekeeping Operation in Angola (UNAVEM III) and requests the Secretary-General to confirm urgently that this has been done;

7. Endorses the recommendation of the Secretary-General that the Special Representative continue to chair the Joint Commission, as established under the Lusaka Protocol, which has proved to be a vital conflict resolution and implementation mechanism;

8. Calls upon the Government of Angola and in particular UNITA to cooperate fully with MONUA and to ensure the freedom of movement and the safety of its personnel;

9. Strongly urges the Government of Angola and in particular UNITA to complete the remaining political aspects of the peace process, including the normalization of State administration throughout the national territory according to a timetable and procedures agreed upon by both parties within the context of the Joint Commission, the transformation of the UNITA radio station into a non-partisan broadcasting facility, and the transformation of UNITA into a political party;

10. Also strongly urges the Government of Angola and in particular UNITA to complete without delay the remaining military aspects of the peace process, including the registration and demobilization of all remaining military elements, the elimination of all obstacles to the free circulation of people and goods, and the disarmament of the civilian population;

11. Appeals in the strongest terms to both parties to refrain from any use of force which could obstruct the full implementation of the peace process;

12. Calls upon the Government of Angola to notify MONUA of any troop movements, in accordance with the provisions of the Lusaka Protocol;

13. Demands that UNITA provide to the Joint Commission without delay complete information regarding all armed personnel under its control, including the security detachment of the Leader of the Largest Opposition Party, the so-called "mining police", armed UNITA personnel returning from outside the national boundaries, and any other armed UNITA personnel not previously reported to the United Nations, in order for them to be verified, disarmed and demobilized in accordance with the Lusaka Protocol and agreements between the parties in the context of the Joint

Commission;

14. **Expresses its hope** that the issues now delaying the full implementation of the Lusaka Protocol may be resolved through a meeting, within the national territory, between the President of Angola and the Leader of the Largest Opposition Party;

15. **Urges** the international community to provide assistance to facilitate the demobilization and social reintegration of ex-combatants, the resettlement of displaced persons, and the rehabilitation and reconstruction of the Angolan national economy in order to consolidate the gains in the peace process;

16. **Expresses its appreciation** to the Secretary-General, his Special Representative, and the UNAVEM III personnel for assisting the parties in Angola to implement the peace process;

17. **Decides** to remain actively seized of the matter.

3795th meeting
30 June 1997

S/RES/1125 (MISAB)

The Security Council,

Concerned by the grave crisis facing the Central African Republic,

Taking note with appreciation of the signing of the Bangui Agreements (S/1997/561, Appendixes III-VI) of 25 January 1997 and the creation of the Inter-African Mission to Monitor the Implementation of the Bangui Agreements (MISAB),

Concerned by the fact that, in the Central African Republic, former mutineers, members of militias and other persons continue to bear arms in contravention of the Bangui Agreements,

Taking note of the letter dated 4 July 1997 from the President of the Central African Republic to the Secretary-General (S/1997/561, annex),

Taking note also of the letter dated 7 July 1997 to the Secretary-General from the President of Gabon, on behalf of the members of the International Committee for the follow-up of the Bangui Agreements (S/1997/543),

Determining that the situation in the Central African Republic continues to constitute a threat to international peace and security in the region,

1. **Welcomes** the efforts of the Member States which participate in MISAB and of those Member States which support them;

2. **Approves** the continued conduct by Member States participating in MISAB of the operation in a neutral and impartial way to achieve its objective to facilitate the return to peace and security by monitoring the implementation of the Bangui Agreements in the Central African Republic as stipulated in the mandate of MISAB (S/1997/561, Appendix I), including through the supervision of the surrendering of arms of former mutineers, militias and all other persons unlawfully bearing arms;

3. **Acting** under Chapter VII of the Charter of the United Nations, authorizes the Member States participating in MISAB and those States providing logistical support to ensure the security and freedom of movement of their personnel;

4. **Decides** that the authorization referred to in paragraph 3 above will be limited to an initial period of three months from the adoption of this resolution, at which time the Council will assess the situation on the basis of the reports referred to in paragraph 6 below;

5. Stresses that the expenses and logistical support for the force will be borne on a voluntary basis in accordance with article 11 of the mandate of MISAB;

6. Requests the Member States participating in MISAB to provide periodic reports at least every two weeks through the Secretary-General, the first report to be made within 14 days after the adoption of this resolution;

7. Decides to remain actively seized of the matter.

3808th meeting
6 August 1997

S/RES/1136 (MISAB)

The Security Council,

Reaffirming its resolution 1125 (1997) of 6 August 1997,

Taking note of the sixth report to the Council by the International Committee for the follow-up of the Bangui Agreements (S/1997/828, annex),

Taking note of the letter dated 17 October 1997 from the President of the Central African Republic to the Secretary-General (S/1997/840, annex),

Taking note further of the letter dated 23 October 1997 to the President of the Security Council from the President of Gabon, on behalf of the members of the International Committee for the follow-up of the Bangui Agreements (S/1997/821, annex)

Expressing appreciation for the neutral and impartial way in which the Inter-African Mission to Monitor the Implementation of the Bangui Agreements (MISAB) has carried out its mandate, in close cooperation with the Central African authorities and noting with satisfaction that MISAB has contributed to stabilizing the situation in the Central African Republic, in particular through the supervision of the surrendering of arms,

Noting that the States participating in MISAB and the Central African Republic have decided to extend its mandate (S/1997/561, appendix I) in order to complete its mission,

Stressing the importance of regional stability and, in this context, fully supporting the efforts made by the Member States participating in the International Mediation Committee established by the Nineteenth Summit Meeting of Heads of State and Government of France and Africa, and by the members of the International Committee for the follow-up of the Bangui Agreements,

Stressing also the need for all signatories of the Bangui Agreements to continue to cooperate fully in respecting and implementing these Agreements,

Determining that the situation in the Central African Republic continues to constitute a threat to international peace and security in the region,

1. Welcomes the efforts made by the Member States which participate in MISAB and of those Member States which provide support to them, and their readiness to maintain these efforts;

2. Welcomes the support provided by the United Nations Development Programme to the International Committee for the follow-up of the Bangui Agreements and encourages it to continue this support;

3. Approves the continued conduct by Member States participating in MISAB of the operation in a neutral and impartial way to achieve its objective as set out in paragraph 2 of resolution 1125 (1997);

4. Acting under Chapter VII of the

the Member States participating in MISAB and those States providing logistical support to ensure the security and freedom of movement of their personnel;

5. Decides that the authorization referred to in paragraph 4 above will be limited to a period of three months from the adoption of this resolution;

6. Recalls that the expenses and logistical support for MISAB will be borne on a voluntary basis in accordance with article 11 of the mandate of MISAB, requests the Secretary-General to take the necessary steps to establish a Trust Fund for the Central African Republic which would assist in supporting the troops of States participating in MISAB and in providing logistical support to them, and encourages Member States to contribute to the Trust Fund;

7. Requests the Member States participating in MISAB to provide periodic reports to the Council at least every month through the Secretary-General, the next report to be made within one month of the adoption of this resolution;

8. Requests the Secretary-General to provide a report before the end of the three-month period referred to in paragraph 5 above, on the implementation of this resolution, including recommendations on further international support for the Central African Republic;

9. Urges all States, international organizations and financial institutions to assist in post-conflict development in the Central African Republic;

10. Decides to remain actively seized of the matter.

3829th meeting
6 November 1997

> "I have recently taken measures to strengthen the International Tribunal for Rwanda and ensure that those responsible for the genocide and other crimes committed during the tragic conflict in that country in 1994 are brought to justice.
>
> We must put an end to impunity so that yesterday's injustices do not become tomorrow's problems. The many peace efforts now under way cannot succeed without the unfailing political will of the central African states themselves."
>
> **Kofi A. Annan**
> **Secretary-General of the United Nations**
> **7 July 1997**

List of Meetings

*dealing with the UN Standing Advisory Committee
on Security Questions in Central Africa*

Meeting	Venue		Date	Document
Conference on Confidence-Building, Security and Development Within the Framework of the Economic Community of Central African States	Lomé, Togo		15-19 February 1988	United Nations Regional Centre for Peace and Disarmament in Africa Conference Report # 2
Organizational Meeting	Yaoundé, Cameroon		27-31 July 1992	A/47/511
Second Ministerial Meeting	Bujumbura, Burundi	experts ministers	8-10 March 1993 11-12 March 1993	A/48/412
Third Ministerial Meeting	Libreville, Gabon	experts ministers	30 Aug.-1 Sept. 1993 2-3 Sept. 1993	A/48/412
Fourth Ministerial Meeting	Yaoundé, Cameroon	experts ministers	4-6 April 1994 7-8 April 1994	A/49/546
Fifth Ministerial Meeting	Yaoundé, Cameroon	experts ministers	5-7 Sept. 1994 8-9 Sept. 1994	A/49/546
Sixth Ministerial Meeting	Brazzaville, Congo	experts ministers	20-22 March 1995 23-24 March 1995	A/50/474
Seventh Ministerial Meeting	Brazzaville, Congo	experts ministers	28 Aug.-30 Aug. 1995 31 Aug.-1 Sept. 1995	A/50/474
Eighth Ministerial Meeting	Yaoundé, Cameroon	experts ministers	15-17 April 1996 18-19 April 1996	A/51/287
Bureau Meeting	Brazzaville, Congo		14-15 June 1996	
First Summit Meeting of Heads of State & Gov't. (signing of Non-Aggression Pact)	Yaoundé, Cameroon		8 July 1996	A/51/274-S/1996/631
First Training Seminar on Peace Operations	Yaoundé, Cameroon		9-17 Sept. 1996	
Second Summit Meeting of Heads of State & Gov't.	Brazzaville, Cameroon		2-3 Dec. 1996	S/1996/1006
Ninth Ministerial Meeting	Libreville, Gabon		7-11 July 1997	A/52/293 and A/52/283*-S/1997/644*

Participation of Central African States in Multilateral Disarmament Treaties
(as of 17 September 1997)

(s) signed; (r) ratified (including accessions and successions)

Signatory or party reported	Geneva Protocol[1]	Partial Test Ban[2]	Outer Space[3]	NPT[4]	CTBT[5]	Sea-Bed[6]	BW[7]	CWC[8]	ENMOD[9]	Pelindaba Treaty[10]
Angola	r			r	s					s
Burundi		s	s	r	s	s	s	s		s
Cameroon	r	s	s	s r		s		s r		s
Central African Republic	r	r	s	r		s r	s	s		s
Chad		s r		s r	s			s		s
Congo				r	s	r	r	s		s
Dem. Rep. of the Congo (Zaire)		s r	s	s r	s		s r	s	s	s
Equatorial Guinea	r	r	r	r	s	s	r	s r		
Gabon		s r		r	s		s	s		s
Rwanda	r	s r	s	r		s r	s r	s		s
Sao Tome & Principe				r	s	r	r		r	s

1 **Protocol for the Prohibition of the Use of War of Asphyxiating, Poisonous or Other Gases, and of Bacteriological Methods of Warfare**
Signed at Geneva: 17 June 1925
Entered into force: for each signatory as from the date of deposit of its ratification; accessions take effect on the date of the notification by the depositary Government.
Depositary Government: France

2 **Treaty Banning Nuclear Weapon Tests in the Atmosphere, in Outer Space and under Water**
Signed by the original parties at Moscow: 5 August 1963
Opened for signature at London, Moscow and Washington: 8 August 1963
Entered into force: 10 October 1963
Depositary Governments: Russian Federation, United Kingdom of Great Britain and Northern Ireland and United States of America

3 **Treaty on Principles Governing the Activities of States in the Exploration and Use of Outer Space, including the Moon and Other Celestial Bodies**
Opened for signature at London, Moscow and Washington: 27 January 1967
Entered into force: 10 October 1967
Depositary Governments: Russian Federation, United Kingdom of Great Britain and Northern Ireland and United States of America

4 **Treaty on the Non-Proliferation of Nuclear Weapons**
Opened for signature at London, Moscow and Washington: 1 July 1968
Entered into force: 5 March 1970
Depositary Governments: Russian Federation, United Kingdom of Great Britain and Northern Ireland and United States of America

Abréviations et sigles

CEEAC	Communauté économique des Etats d'Afrique centrale
CEPGL	Communauté économique des pays des Grands Lacs
CSSA	Conseil supérieur du sport en Afrique
FAA	forces armées angolaises
FPR	Front patriotique rwandais
GOMN	Groupe d'observateurs militaires neutres
GONUBA	Groupe d'observation des Nations Unies dans la bande d'Aouzou
MINUAR	Mission des Nations Unies pour l'assistance au Rwanda
MISAB	Mission interafricaine de surveillance des accords de Bangui
MONUA	Mission d'observation des Nations Unies en Angola
MONUOR	Mission d'observation des Nations Unies Ouganda-Rwanda
MPLA	Mouvement populaire de la libération de l'Angola
ONUC	Opération des Nations Unies au Congo
OTAN	Organisation du traité de l'Atlantique Nord
OUA	Organisation de l'Unité africaine
PNUD	Programme des Nations Unies pour le développement
UDEAC	Union économique et douanière de l'Afrique centrale
UNAVEM	Mission de vérification des Nations Unies en Angola
UNITA	União Nacional para a Independência Total de Angola

Litho in United Nations, New York
31522—December 1997—4,685

Abbreviations and Acronyms

CACEU	Central African Customs and Economic Union
CEPGL	Economic Community of the Great Lakes Countries
ECCAS	Economic Community of Central African States
FAA	Angolan Armed Forces
MISAB	Inter-African Mission to Monitor the Implementation of the Bangui Agreements
MONUA	United Nations Observer Mission in Angola
MPLA	Movimento Popular para a Libertacao de Angola (Popular Movement for the Liberation of Angola)
NATO	North Atlantic Treaty Organization
NMOG II	Neutral Military Observer Group
OAU	Organization of African Unity
ONUC	United Nations Operation in the Congo
RPF	Rwandese Patriotic Front
SCSA	Supreme Council for Sport in Africa
UNAMIR	United Nations Assistance Mission for Rwanda
UNASOG	United Nations Aouzou Strip Observer Group
UNAVEM	United Nations Angola Verification Mission
UNDP	United Nations Development Programme
UNITA	União Nacional para a Independência Total de Angola (National Union for the Total Independence of Angola)
UNOMUR	United Nations Observer Mission Uganda-Rwanda

5 Comprehensive Nuclear-Test-Ban Treaty
Opened for signature at New York: 24 September 1996
Not yet in force
Depositary: The Secretary-General of the United Nations

6 Treaty on the Prohibition of the Emplacement of Nuclear Weapons and Other Weapons of Mass Destruction on the Sea-Bed and the Ocean Floor and in the Subsoil Thereof
Opened for signature at London, Moscow and Washington: 11 February 1971
Entered into force: 18 May 1972
Depositary Governments: Russian Federation, United Kingdom of Great Britain and Northern Ireland and United States of America

7 Convention on the Prohibition of the Development, Production and Stockpiling of Bacteriological (Biological) and Toxin Weapons and on Their Destruction
Opened for signature at London, Moscow and Washington: 10 April 1972
Entered into force: 26 March 1975
Depositary Governments: Russian Federation, United Kingdom of Great Britain and Northern Ireland and United States of America

8 Convention on the Prohibition of the Development, Production, Stockpiling and Use of Chemical Weapons and on Their Destruction
Opened for signature at Paris: 13 January 1993
Entered into force: 29 April 1997
Depositary: The Secretary-General of the United Nations

9 Convention on the Prohibition of Military or Any Other Hostile Use of Environmental Modification Techniques
Opened for signature at Geneva: 18 May 1977
Entered into force: 5 October 1978
Depositary: The Secretary-General of the United Nations

10 African Nuclear-Weapon-Free-Zone Treaty
Opened for signature at Cairo: 11 April 1996
Not yet in force
Depositary: The Secretary-General of the Organization of African Unity

-----